C000004000

The Complete Slow Cooker Cookbook

1600 Days of Savory and Satisfying Slow Cooker Recipes to Nourish Your Body

Shelly J. Wilkerson

Copyright© 2023 By Shelly J. Wilkerson Rights Reserved

This book is copyright protected. It is only for personal use. You cannot amend, distribute, sell, use, quote or paraphrase any part of the content within this book, without the consent of the author or publisher.

Under no circumstances will any blame or legal responsibility be held against the publisher, or author, for any damages, reparation, or monetary loss due to the information contained within this book, either directly or indirectly.

Disclaimer Notice:

Please note the information contained within this document is for educational and entertainment purposes only. All effort has been executed to present accurate, up to date, reliable, complete information. No warranties of any kind are declared or implied. Readers acknowledge that the author is not engaged in the rendering of legal, financial, medical or professional advice. The content within this book has been derived from various sources. Please consult a licensed professional before attempting any techniques outlined in this book.

By reading this document, the reader agrees that under no circumstances is the author responsible for any losses, direct or indirect, that are incurred as a result of the use of the information contained within this document, including, but not limited to, errors, omissions, or inaccuracies.

Editor: AALIYAH LYONS

Interior Design: BROOKE WHITE

Cover Art: DANIELLE REES

Food stylist: SIENNA ADAMS

Table Of Contents

Introduction

In the hustle and bustle of modern life, the art of slow cooking is a precious gem that many of us have, regrettably, lost sight of. In our quest for efficiency and speed, we often forget the unmatched joy of savoring a lovingly prepared, slow-cooked meal that has simmered for hours, filling our homes with warmth and our hearts with anticipation. But this cookbook, "The Complete Slow Cooker Cookbook," seeks to rekindle that love affair with the slow cooker, inviting you on a culinary journey that celebrates the power of patience and the magic of simplicity.

The slow cooker, often affectionately referred to as a "crockpot," is more than just a kitchen appliance. It's a time machine that transports you to a simpler era, a tool that allows you to embrace the pleasure of a leisurely meal, and a trusted companion that takes care of the cooking while you focus on life's other demands. With "The Complete Slow Cooker Cookbook," you'll rediscover the art of slow cooking and its myriad of delights.

This cookbook is a labor of love, a tribute to the rich tapestry of flavors that the slow cooker can weave. It's a collection of recipes that will inspire you, from comforting stews that warm your soul on a chilly winter's evening to tender meats that melt in your mouth, and vibrant vegetarian dishes that prove the slow cooker is a versatile kitchen companion. As you flip through these pages, you'll find that slow cooking isn't just about saving time; it's about enriching your life.

"The Complete Slow Cooker Cookbook" is designed with both beginners and seasoned slow-cooking enthusiasts in mind. If you're new to this art, fear not, for the book is your gentle guide into the world of slow cooking. You'll learn the basics, including essential tips, techniques, and the benefits of using a slow cooker in your kitchen. For the veterans, there's a treasure trove of inventive recipes that will rekindle your passion and inspire you to explore new horizons in slow cooking.

Every recipe in this book has been crafted with precision and a deep love for the culinary arts. Each ingredient, each measurement, and each step has been carefully considered to ensure that your slow-cooked creations are nothing short of exceptional. The collection spans various cuisines and dietary preferences, so whether you're a fan of classic comfort food, a lover of international flavors, or a health-conscious eater, you'll find dishes that cater to your palate.

Beyond the recipes, "The Complete Slow Cooker Cookbook" embraces the spirit of community, sharing, and family. The aroma of a slow-cooked meal wafting through the house has a remarkable way of bringing people together. It sparks conversations, creates cherished memories, and strengthens the bonds between family and friends. This book celebrates the idea of gathering around the table, sharing stories, and enjoying nourishing, delicious food together.

As you embark on your slow cooking journey with this cookbook, you'll realize that the slow cooker is not just a kitchen tool but a partner in nurturing yourself and your loved ones. It's a tool that allows you to prepare meals with intention and care, no matter how busy life gets. It's a reminder that the best things in life are worth waiting for, that the simple act of cooking can be a source of joy and fulfillment.

I hope this book rekindles your passion for the art of slow cooking, that it encourages you to savor every moment of the process, and that it fills your kitchen with delightful aromas that welcome you home after a long day. "The Complete Slow Cooker Cookbook" is more than a collection of recipes; it's an invitation to slow down, to reconnect with the joy of cooking, and to embrace the warmth and comfort of homemade meals.

So, get ready to embark on a culinary adventure that is not only delicious but also deeply rewarding. Your slow cooker is your trusted ally, and this cookbook is your roadmap to a world of flavors and possibilities. With every dish you create, you'll be celebrating the art of slow cooking, and I can't wait to hear about the delightful meals and memories you'll create along the way.

Happy slow cooking!

Chapter 1

Rediscovering the Art of Slow Cooking

Mastering the Art of Slow Cooking

The slow cooker, often affectionately known as a "crockpot," is a remarkable kitchen appliance that has revolutionized meal preparation for busy individuals, families, and culinary enthusiasts. It's a versatile device designed to simplify the cooking process, enhance flavors, and provide a convenient solution for those seeking nourishing, delicious meals without the need for constant monitoring and supervision.

HOW DOES A SLOW COOKER WORK?

At its core, a slow cooker is an electrical appliance that applies low and consistent heat to your ingredients over an extended period. This gentle simmering gradually tenderizes tough cuts of meat, melds flavors together, and transforms even the most basic ingredients into rich, flavorful dishes. Most slow cookers consist of the following components:

- The Base Unit: This unit contains the heating element that produces the necessary heat to cook your meal. It typically has adjustable temperature settings, allowing you to control the cooking process.
- The Cooking Pot (Insert): The insert is where your ingredients are placed. It's usually made of ceramic or metal and is designed to distribute heat evenly. Some inserts can be used on the stovetop for searing or browning before slow cooking.
- The Lid: The lid fits tightly over the cooking pot, sealing in moisture and heat. This helps to prevent heat loss and ensures your ingredients cook uniformly.

Benefits of Using a Slow Cooker

The slow cooker, also known as a crockpot, is more than just a kitchen appliance; it's a game-changer that has found its way into the hearts and homes of countless cooks. Its rise to culinary fame is no accident, as it brings a host of benefits that can revolutionize the way you prepare and enjoy meals. Let's explore the manifold advantages of using a slow cooker and how it can transform your kitchen experience.

CONVENIENCE AND TIME-SAVING

1. One of the most prominent benefits of a slow cooker is the convenience it offers. It simplifies meal preparation, allowing you to assemble your ingredients in the morning and return to a fully-cooked, hot meal in the evening. This is a life-saver for those with busy schedules and little time to devote to cooking.

FLAVOR ENHANCEMENT

2. Slow cooking is a magical process that enhances the flavors of your dishes. The long, slow simmering allows ingredients to meld, creating deep, complex flavors. Tough cuts of meat become tender, and herbs and spices infuse the entire dish with their essence.

HEALTHIER COOKING

3. Slow cooking typically requires less fat and oil than other cooking methods. The extended cooking time allows flavors to develop without relying on excess fats. Additionally, the low and slow approach preserves the nutritional value of ingredients, making slow-cooked meals not only delicious but also healthy.

VERSATILITY

4. Slow cookers are versatile kitchen companions. You can prepare a wide variety of dishes, from soups and stews to roasts, casseroles, and even des-

serts. Whether you're a fan of comforting classics or exotic flavors, your slow cooker can handle it all.

MONEY-SAVING

5. Using less expensive cuts of meat is a budget-friendly approach to slow cooking. These cuts benefit from slow, gentle cooking and become exceptionally tender and flavorful. Slow cooking allows you to create gourmet-level meals without the gourmet price tag.

MINIMAL SUPERVISION

6. Unlike traditional cooking methods that require constant attention and monitoring, slow cooking demands minimal supervision. Once your ingredients are in the pot, you can go about your day, returning to a ready meal when it's time to eat.

TENDER MEATS

7. For meat lovers, the slow cooker is a treasure trove of tender, succulent cuts. Tough meats, like brisket or shoulder, are transformed into melt-in-the-mouth delicacies, perfect for hearty sandwiches, tacos, or roasts.

EFFICIENT USE OF ENERGY

8. Slow cookers are energy-efficient appliances. They consume less energy compared to ovens and stovetops, making them an environmentally friendly choice. Their enclosed design retains heat, cooking your meal with minimal heat loss.

NO MORE PREHEATING

9. Unlike ovens, slow cookers don't require preheating. You can start cooking immediately, saving both time and energy.

LESS KITCHEN HEAT

10. During hot summer months, slow cookers keep your kitchen cool. You won't have to worry about a sweltering kitchen while preparing a hot meal, making them perfect for year-round use.

MULTIPLE SERVINGS AND LEFTOVERS

11. Slow cookers are great for batch cooking. You can prepare larger quantities and enjoy leftovers for subsequent meals. This is especially convenient for busy families or individuals who prefer meal prepping.

EASY CLEANUP

12. Cleaning a slow cooker is a breeze. Most models have removable, dishwasher-safe inserts, making post-meal cleanup quick and hassle-free.

Guiding Principles for Slow Cooking

Slow cooking is an art, a method that transforms basic ingredients into extraordinary dishes through the power of time and patience. To master this culinary craft, it's essential to embrace a set of guiding principles that unlock the full potential of your slow cooker and infuse your meals with rich flavors and tender textures. Let's delve into these key principles that will elevate your slow cooking to a new level of excellence.

INGREDIENT SELECTION: QUALITY MATTERS

1. The heart of every slow-cooked masterpiece lies in the ingredients you choose. Opt for fresh, high-quality ingredients, from meats and vegetables to spices and herbs. While slow cooking can work wonders with less expensive cuts of meat, investing in good quality can elevate your dish further.

PREP WITH PRECISION

2.   Preparation is key to a successful slow-cooked meal. Thoroughly trim and season your meats. Chop your vegetables evenly to ensure even cooking. Don't forget to sear or brown ingredients when applicable, as this step enhances the flavor and texture of your final creation.

LAYERING FOR FLAVOR

3.   When using a slow cooker, consider layering ingredients thoughtfully. Hearty vegetables and proteins can be layered in a manner that ensures all components receive even heat and flavor distribution. For optimal results, place denser ingredients at the bottom and lighter ones on top.

LIQUID MAGIC

4.   Liquids play a pivotal role in slow cooking. Broth, wine, sauces, and aromatic infusions infuse dishes with flavor. Be mindful of the quantity of liquid you use, as too much can result in a soupy consistency, while too little can lead to dryness.

LOW AND SLOW: THE RIGHT TEMPERATURE

5.   The essence of slow cooking is in the name itself. The low and slow approach is a cornerstone of success. Cooking on low heat allows flavors to meld and ingredients to tenderize, ensuring a sublime culinary experience. Some dishes may require a period of high heat at the start for searing or browning, but they should transition to a low setting for the majority of the cooking time.

TIMING IS EVERYTHING

6.   Time is your ally in slow cooking. While you may be tempted to check your dish frequently, trust the process and let your slow cooker work its magic. Slow-cooked meals often require several hours, so patience is a virtue.

DON'T OVERFILL THE POT

7.   Avoid overloading your slow cooker. For the best results, it's advisable to fill the cooker no more than two-thirds full. Overfilling can lead to uneven cooking and compromised texture.

MINIMAL PEEKING

8.   Resist the urge to frequently lift the lid and peek at your dish. Every time the lid is removed, heat escapes, and the cooking time is extended. Instead, trust that your meal is progressing beautifully under the lid.

FINISHING TOUCHES

9.   Towards the end of the cooking time, consider adding fresh herbs, aromatic spices, or a dash of cream to add a burst of flavor and freshness to your dish. These finishing touches can elevate your meal from delicious to extraordinary.

TASTE AND ADJUST

10.   Before serving, taste your creation and adjust the seasoning if necessary. A pinch of salt, a dash of acid (like a squeeze of lemon), or a sprinkle of herbs can balance and enhance the flavors.

Chapter 2

Sauces and Condiments

Bordelaise Sauce

Prep time: 15 minutes |Cook time: 8 to 10 hours|
Serves 4

- 1 tablespoon unsalted butter
- 1 small onion, minced
- 2 garlic cloves, minced
- 5 tablespoons all-purpose flour, divided
- 1½ pounds beef marrow bones
- 1 cup Beef Bone Broth (here) or low-sodium if store-bought
- ½ teaspoon kosher salt, plus more for seasoning
- ¼ teaspoon freshly ground black pepper, plus more for seasoning
- ⅓ cup dry red wine, such as Bordeaux
- 1 tablespoon Worcestershire sauce
- 2 bay leaves
- 2 fresh thyme sprigs

1. In a slow cooker with a stove-top function, or in a Dutch oven or heavy-bottomed pan on the stove over medium heat, melt the butter. Add the onion and garlic and sauté until translucent, stirring occasionally, about 10 minutes. Add 2 tablespoons of flour and stir to combine. Continue cooking for another 2 minutes to eliminate the raw taste of the flour.
2. Put the onion and garlic in the slow cooker, along with the marrow bones, broth, salt, pepper, wine, Worcestershire sauce, bay leaves, and thyme and cook on low for 8 to 10 hours.
3. About 1 hour before serving, transfer ¼ cup of sauce to a small bowl. Whisk the sauce with the remaining 3 tablespoons of flour until no lumps remain. (If the sauté step was omitted, whisk in the full 5 tablespoons of flour.) Pour the mixture back into the slow cooker. Cover and continue cooking until the sauce begins to thicken.
4. Using a fine-mesh sieve or cheesecloth-lined colander, strain the sauce and discard the solids. Season with additional salt and pepper, if needed. Use immediately or cover and store in the refrigerator for up to 3 days.

Enchilada Sauce

Prep time: 10 minutes | Cook time: 7 to 8 hours on low | Makes 4 cups

- ¼ cup extra-virgin olive oil, divided
- 2 cups puréed tomatoes
- 1 cup water
- 1 sweet onion, chopped
- 2 jalapeño peppers, chopped
- 2 teaspoons minced garlic
- 2 tablespoons chili powder
- 1 teaspoon ground coriander

1. Lightly grease the insert of the slow cooker with 1 tablespoon of the olive oil.
2. Place the remaining 3 tablespoons of the olive oil, tomatoes, water, onion, jalapeño peppers, garlic, chili powder, and coriander in the insert.
3. Cover and cook on low 7 to 8 hours.
4. Serve over poultry or meat. After cooling, store the sauce in a sealed container in the refrigerator for up to 1 week.

Fresh Tomato Sauce

Prep time: 10 minutes | Cook time: 20 minutes |
Makes about 3 cups

- 2 pounds ripe plum tomatoes, peeled cored, halved, and seeded
- 4 garlic cloves, smashed and peeled
- ¼ cup extra-virgin olive oil
- 4 to 5 basil sprigs
- 1 teaspoon coarse salt, plus more to taste
- ¼ teaspoon freshly ground pepper
- pinch sugar
- ½ cup boiling water

1. Preheat a 5- to 6-quart slow cooker. Add tomatoes, garlic, oil, basil, salt, pepper, and sugar to the slow cooker; stir to combine.
2. Add the boiling water. Cover and cook on high until sauce thickens slightly, 1 hour. Reduce heat to low and cook 4 hours.
3. For a thicker sauce, continue cooking on low for 2 hours, or until desired thickness is reached.
4. Use sauce immediately, or let cool to room temperature and refrigerate in an airtight container up to 3 days.

Marinara Sauce

Prep time: 20 minutes | Cook time: 6-8 hours |
Makes 12 cups

- 4 pounds Roma tomatoes, chopped
- 4 beefsteak tomatoes, seeded and chopped
- 1 6-ounce can BPA-free tomato paste
- 2 onions, peeled and chopped
- 4 garlic cloves, peeled and minced
- ½ cup shredded carrot
- 1 bay leaf
- 2 teaspoons dried basil leaves
- 1 teaspoon dried oregano leaves

1. In a 6-quart slow cooker, mix all the ingredients. Cover and cook on low for 6 to 8 hours.
2. Remove and discard the bay leaf.
3. You can freeze this sauce as is, or you can puree it by using a potato masher to crush some of the tomatoes.
4. Divide the sauce into 2-cup portions and freeze up to 4 months.

Barbecue Sauce

Prep time: 10 minutes | Cook time: 20 minutes |
Makes 4 cups

- 2 tablespoons safflower or canola oil
- 1 onion, finely chopped
- 3 garlic cloves, minced
- coarse salt and freshly ground pepper
- 1¼ teaspoons chili powder
- 1 can (28 ounces) whole peeled tomatoes, pureed with their juices
- ¾ cup water, plus more as needed
- ¼ cup packed dark brown sugar
- ¼ cup ketchup
- 2 tablespoons apple cider vinegar

1. Preheat a 5- to 6-quart slow cooker.
2. Heat oil in a saucepan over medium-high. Add onion, garlic, 1 teaspoon salt, and ½ teaspoon pepper, and cook until onion is translucent, about 5 minutes. Stir in chili powder and cook until fragrant, about 1 minute.
3. Transfer onion mixture to the slow cooker. Add tomatoes, the water, brown sugar, and ketchup. Cover and cook on high for 3 hours (or on low for 6 hours). Let cool slightly.
4. Transfer sauce to a blender and puree. Stir in vinegar; season with salt and pepper. Let cool completely. (Barbecue sauce can be refrigerated in an airtight container up to 2 weeks.)

Alfredo Sauce

Prep time: 10 minutes |Cook time: 4 to 6 hours|
Serves 4

- Cooking spray or 1 tablespoon extra-virgin olive oil
- ½ quart heavy (whipping) cream
- ¼ cup Chicken Stock (here) or low-sodium if store-bought
- ¼ cup butter, melted
- 2 garlic cloves, minced
- 1 cup finely shredded Parmesan cheese, plus more for garnish
- 2 tablespoons dry sherry
- ¾ teaspoon kosher salt, plus more for seasoning
- ½ teaspoon freshly ground black pepper, plus more for seasoning
- 3 tablespoons all-purpose flour

1. Use the cooking spray or olive oil to coat the inside (bottom and sides) of the slow cooker. Add the cream, chicken stock, butter, garlic, Parmesan, sherry, salt, and pepper and whisk to combine. Cover and cook on low for 4 to 6 hours.
2. About 30 minutes before serving, whisk in the flour. Leave the lid ajar and continue cooking until the sauce begins to thicken. Season with additional salt and pepper, if needed. Serve on pasta, passing additional Parmesan to sprinkle on top.

Classic Italian Meat Sauce

Prep time: 10 minutes | Cook time: 6 to 8 hours |
Serves 4

- 1/2 cup olive oil
- 2 medium-size yellow onions, chopped
- 2 medium-size carrots, finely chopped
- 2 ribs celery, finely chopped
- 1 pound lean ground beef
- Salt and freshly ground black pepper to taste
- 1 1/2 cups dry red wine, such as Chianti
- Two 28-ounce cans whole plum tomatoes, with their juice; or 2 pounds fresh ripe plum tomatoes, peeled, seeded, and cut into chunks
- One 6-ounce can tomato paste
- 1/2 cup beef broth

1. Heat the oil in a large skillet over medium heat. Cook the onions, carrots, and celery, stirring occasionally, until just browned, 10 to 15 minutes. Add the beef and cook until no longer pink; season with salt and pepper.
2. Transfer to the slow cooker. Add the wine to the pan over high heat and cook, scraping up any browned bits stuck to the bottom, until it reduces to half its volume. Pour into the slow cooker and add the tomatoes, tomato paste, and broth. Cover and cook on LOW for 6 to 8 hours. Serve the sauce hot. It will keep in the refrigerator up to 4 days and in the freezer for a month.

Roasted Tomato Sauce

Prep time: 20 minutes | Cook time: 9-11 hours |
Makes 13 cups sauce

- 4 pounds Roma tomatoes, seeded and chopped
- 2 onions, chopped
- 5 garlic cloves, minced
- 3 tablespoons extra-virgin olive oil
- 2 cups bottled tomato juice
- 3 tablespoons tomato paste
- 2 teaspoons dried basil leaves
- ½ teaspoon salt
- ⅛ teaspoon white pepper

1. In a 6-quart slow cooker, place all the tomatoes. Partially cover the slow cooker and cook the tomatoes on high for 3 hours, stirring the tomatoes twice during cooking time.
2. Add the remaining ingredients. Cover and cook on low for 6 to 8 hours longer, until the sauce is bubbling and the consistency you want.
3. You can make the sauce smoother if you'd like by working the sauce with a potato masher, or leave it as is.
4. Divide the sauce into 2-cup portions and freeze up to 3 months.

Queso Sauce

Prep time: 10 minutes | Cook time: 3 to 4 hours
on low | Makes 4 cups

- 1 tablespoon extra-virgin olive oil
- 12 ounces cream cheese
- 1 cup sour cream
- 2 cups salsa verde
- 1 cup monterey jack cheese, shredded

1. Lightly grease the insert of the slow cooker with the olive oil.
2. In a large bowl, stir together the cream cheese, sour cream, salsa verde, and Monterey Jack cheese, until blended.
3. Transfer the mixture to the insert.
4. Cover and cook on low for 3 to 4 hours.
5. Serve warm.

Hot Crab Sauce

Prep time: 10 minutes | Cook time: 5 to 6 hours
on low | Makes 4 cups

- 8 ounces cream cheese
- 8 ounces goat cheese
- 1 cup sour cream
- ½ cup grated asiago cheese
- 1 sweet onion, finely chopped
- 1 tablespoon granulated erythritol
- 2 teaspoons minced garlic
- 12 ounces crabmeat, flaked
- 1 scallion, white and green parts, chopped

1. In a large bowl, stir together the cream cheese, goat cheese, sour cream, Asiago cheese, onion, erythritol, garlic, crabmeat, and scallion until well mixed.
2. Transfer the mixture to an 8-by-4-inch loaf pan and place the pan in the insert of the slow cooker.
3. Cover and cook on low for 5 to 6 hours.
4. Serve warm.

Bolognese Sauce

Prep time: 20 minutes | Cook time: 7-9 hours |
Makes 12 cups

- 2 pounds lean grass-fed ground beef
- 2 onions, chopped
- 7 garlic cloves, minced
- 1 large carrot, grated
- ¼ cup tomato paste
- 3 pounds Roma tomatoes, seeded and chopped
- 2 cups bottled tomato juice
- 1 bay leaf
- 1 teaspoon dried oregano leaves
- ½ teaspoon salt

1. In a large skillet, mix the ground beef, onions, and garlic. Cook over medium heat, stirring frequently to break up the meat, until the beef is browned. Drain.
2. In a 6-quart slow cooker, mix the beef mixture with the remaining ingredients. Cover and cook on low for 7 to 9 hours, or until the sauce is thickened.
3. Remove the bay leaf and discard.
4. Divide the sauce into 3-cup portions and freeze up to 3 months. To use, let the sauce thaw in the refrigerator overnight, then slowly heat in a saucepan until the sauce is bubbling.

Creamy Alfredo Sauce

Prep time: 5 minutes | Cook time: 6 hours on low |
Makes 6 cups

- 1 tablespoon extra-virgin olive oil
- 4 cups chicken broth
- 2 cups heavy (whipping) cream
- 3 teaspoons minced garlic
- ½ cup butter
- 1 cup grated parmesan cheese
- 2 tablespoons chopped fresh parsley
- freshly ground black pepper, for seasoning

1. Lightly grease the insert of the slow cooker with the olive oil.
2. Stir in the broth, heavy cream, and garlic until combined.
3. Cover and cook on low for 6 hours.
4. Whisk in the butter, Parmesan cheese, and parsley.
5. Season with pepper and serve.

Buffalo Wing Sauce

Prep time: 5 minutes |Cook time: 6 hours| Serves
3

- 1 (12-ounce) bottle Louisiana-style hot sauce
- ½ cup (1 stick) unsalted butter
- 2 tablespoons Worcestershire sauce
- 2 teaspoons garlic powder
- 2 teaspoons onion powder
- ¼ teaspoon cayenne pepper
- ¼ teaspoon kosher salt, plus more for seasoning
- Freshly ground black pepper

1. To the slow cooker, add the hot sauce, butter, Worcestershire sauce, garlic powder, onion powder, cayenne, and salt. Stir to combine. Cover and cook on low for 6 hours.
2. Season with additional salt and pepper, as needed.

Pepper Steak Sauce

Prep time: 10 minutes |Cook time: 6 hours| Serves 2

- 3 large red peppers, seeded and roughly chopped
- 2 garlic cloves, smashed
- ¼ cup ketchup
- ¼ cup orange juice
- 2 tablespoons tomato paste
- 2 tablespoons Dijon mustard
- 2 tablespoons balsamic vinegar
- 2 tablespoons Worcestershire sauce
- 1 tablespoon brown sugar
- 1 tablespoon raisins
- ½ teaspoon celery seed
- ½ teaspoon kosher salt, plus more for seasoning
- ¼ teaspoon freshly ground black pepper, plus more for seasoning
- 3 tablespoons all-purpose flour

1. To the slow cooker, add the peppers, garlic, ketchup, orange juice, tomato paste, mustard, vinegar, Worcestershire sauce, brown sugar, raisins, celery seed, salt, and pepper. Cover and cook on low for 6 hours.
2. About 1 hour before serving, transfer ¼ cup of sauce to a small bowl. Whisk in the flour until no lumps remain. Pour the mixture into the slow cooker, cover, and continue cooking until the sauce begins to thicken.
3. Season with additional salt and pepper, if needed. Use an immersion blender or transfer to a blender to purée the sauce. Use the sauce immediately, or cover and store in the refrigerator for up to 1 week.

Simple Marinara Sauce

Prep time: 10 minutes | Cook time: 7 to 8 hours on low | Serves 12

- 3 tablespoons extra-virgin olive oil, divided
- 2 (28-ounce) cans crushed tomatoes
- ½ sweet onion, finely chopped
- 2 teaspoons minced garlic
- ½ teaspoon salt
- 1 tablespoon chopped fresh basil
- 1 tablespoon chopped fresh oregano

1. Lightly grease the insert of the slow cooker with 1 tablespoon of the olive oil.
2. Add the remaining 2 tablespoons of the olive oil, tomatoes, onion, garlic, and salt to the insert, stirring to combine.
3. Cover and cook on low for 7 to 8 hours.
4. Remove the cover and stir in the basil and oregano.
5. Store the cooled sauce in a sealed container in the refrigerator for up to 1 week.

Nacho Cheese Sauce

Prep time: 13 minutes |Cook time: 3 hours| Serves 10

- 1 (2-pound) box original Velveeta cheese, cut into chunks
- 8 ounces sharp Cheddar cheese, shredded
- 1 pound hot breakfast sausage, browned
- 1 (4-ounce) can chopped green or red chiles
- 1 teaspoon kosher salt
- 1 teaspoon freshly ground black pepper
- 1 tablespoon chili powder
- 1½ teaspoons ground cumin
- ½ teaspoon onion powder
- ¼ teaspoon garlic powder
- ¼ teaspoon dried oregano
- ¼ teaspoon red pepper flakes

1. To the slow cooker, add the Velveeta and Cheddar, browned sausage, chiles, salt, pepper, chili powder, cumin, onion powder, garlic powder, oregano, and red pepper flakes.
2. Cover and cook on low for 3 hours.

Classic Bolognese Sauce

Prep time: 15 minutes | Cook time: 7 to 8 hours on low | Serves 10

- 3 tablespoons extra-virgin olive oil, divided
- 1 pound ground pork
- ½ pound ground beef
- ½ pound bacon, chopped
- 1 sweet onion, chopped
- 1 tablespoon minced garlic
- 2 celery stalks, chopped
- 1 carrot, chopped
- 2 (28-ounce) cans diced tomatoes
- ½ cup coconut milk
- ¼ cup apple cider vinegar

1. Lightly grease the insert of the slow cooker with 1 tablespoon of the olive oil.
2. In a large skillet over medium-high heat, heat the remaining 2 tablespoons of the olive oil. Add the pork, beef, and bacon, and sauté until cooked through, about 7 minutes.
3. Stir in the onion and garlic and sauté for an additional 2 minutes.
4. Transfer the meat mixture to the insert and add the celery, carrot, tomatoes, coconut milk, and apple cider vinegar.
5. Cover and cook on low for 7 to 8 hours.
6. Serve, or cool completely, and store in the refrigerator in a sealed container for up to 4 days or in the freezer for 1 month.

Chile-Citrus Ketchup

Prep time: 10 minutes | Cook time: 20 minutes | Makes 1 quart

- 1 can (28 ounces) diced tomatoes
- 1 onion, quartered
- 3 garlic cloves, smashed
- 6 tablespoons dark brown sugar
- ¼ cup apple cider vinegar
- 2 teaspoons dry mustard
- pinch ground nutmeg
- ¼ teaspoon ground allspice
- pinch chili powder
- ½ teaspoon finely grated orange zest plus ⅓ cup fresh orange juice
- 2 tablespoons brewed espresso
- 1 dried bay leaf
- 1 fresh habañero chile
- coarse salt and freshly ground pepper

1. Puree tomatoes, onion, garlic, and brown sugar in a food processor.
2. Transfer mixture to a 5- to 6-quart slow cooker.
3. Add vinegar, 1 cup water, mustard, nutmeg, allspice, chili powder, orange zest and juice, espresso, bay leaf, and chile.
4. Cook, uncovered, on high until thickened, 3 to 4 hours.
5. Remove chile.
6. Puree half or whole chile (depending on desired heat) with 1 cup tomato mixture in food processor.
7. Return ketchup to cooker; stir until well blended.
8. Season with salt and pepper.
9. Let cool completely.

Chapter 3

Appetizers and Snacks

Southwest Hot Chip Dip

Prep time: 15 minutes | Cook time: 1½–4 hours | Serves 15–20

- 1 lb. ground beef, browned, crumbled fine, and drained
- 2 15-oz. cans refried beans
- 2 10-oz. cans diced tomatoes and chilies
- 1 pkg. taco seasoning
- 1 lb. Velveeta cheese, cubed

1. Combine ground beef, beans, tomatoes, and taco seasoning in slow cooker.
2. Cover. Cook on Low 3-4 hours, or on High 1½ hours.
3. Add cheese. Stir occasionally. Heat until cheese is melted.
4. Serve with tortilla chips.

Stuffed Spiced Apples

Prep time: 15 minutes | Cook time: 25 minutes | Serves 4

- 4 medium-sized tart cooking apples (like granny smith or braeburn)
- ⅓ cup finely chopped dried figs or raisins
- ½ cup finely chopped walnuts
- ¼ cup packed light brown sugar
- ½ teaspoon apple pie spice or cinnamon
- ¼ cup apple juice
- 1 tablespoon butter, cut into 4 pieces

1. Core the apples. Cut a strip of peel from the top of each apple. Place the apples upright in the slow cooker.
2. In a small bowl, combine figs, walnuts, brown sugar, and apple pie spice. Spoon the mixture into the center of the apples, patting in with a knife or a narrow metal spatula.
3. Pour the apple juice around the apples in the slow cooker.
4. Top each apple with a piece of butter.

5. Cover and cook on low for 4 to 5 hours or on high for 2 to 2½ hours until very tender.
6. Serve warm, with some of the cooking liquid spooned over the apples.

Easy Pizza Appetizers

Prep time: 15 minutes | Cook time: 1 hour | Serves 8

- 1 lb. ground beef
- 1 lb. bulk Italian sausage
- 1 lb. Velveeta cheese, cubed
- 4 tsp. pizza seasoning
- ½ tsp. Worcestershire sauce

5. In a large nonstick skillet, brown beef and sausage until crumbly. Drain.
6. Add remaining ingredients and place mixture in slow cooker.
7. Cover and heat on Low for 1 hour.
8. When thoroughly warmed, offer a small spoon or knife for spreading and serve with party rye bread.

Apple and Dried Fruit Chutney

Prep time: 10 minutes | Cook time: 4 to 5 hours | Serve 4

- 5 large Granny Smith, pippin, Fuji, or other tart cooking apple, peeled, cored, and coarsely chopped
- 1/2 cup chopped dried apricots
- 1/2 cup chopped dried pears
- 1/2 cup chopped dried peaches
- 1/3 cup golden raisins
- 1 chunk fresh ginger, about 2 inches long, peeled and grated
- 5 to 7 cloves garlic, to your taste, mashed
- 2 1/2 cups sugar
- 1 1/4 cups white wine vinegar
- 1 1/2 teaspoons salt
- 1/2 to 1 teaspoon cayenne pepper, to your taste

1. Combine all the ingredients in the slow cooker. Cover and cook on HIGH for 4 to 4 1/2 hours, until it achieves a jam-like consistency.
2. Remove the lid and let the chutney cook on HIGH an additional 30 minutes to evaporate excess juice and thicken, if necessary.
3. Turn off the cooker and let cool to room temperature in the slow cooker. Scrape with a rubber spatula into clean spring-top glass jars (or use screw tops with new lids). Store, covered, in the refrigerator for 2 weeks before using to allow the flavors to mellow. It will keep in the fridge for up to 2 months. Serve cold or at room temperature.

Slow-Cooked Smokies

Prep time: 5 minutes | Cook time: 6-7 hours | Serves 12-16

- 2 lbs. miniature smoked sausage links

- 28-oz. bottle barbecue sauce
- 1¼ cups water
- 3 tbsp. Worcestershire sauce
- 3 tbsp. steak sauce
- ½ tsp. Pepper

1. In a slow cooker, combine all ingredients. Mix well.
2. Cover and cook on Low 6-7 hours.

Apple French Toast Bake

Prep time: 20 minutes | Cook time: 4-5 hours | Serves 8

- ¼ cup coconut sugar
- 1 teaspoon ground cinnamon
- ¼ teaspoon ground cardamom
- 10 slices whole-wheat bread, cubed
- 2 Granny Smith apples, peeled and diced
- 8 eggs
- 1 cup canned coconut milk
- 1 cup unsweetened apple juice
- 2 teaspoons vanilla extract
- 1 cup granola

1. Grease a 6-quart slow cooker with plain vegetable oil.
2. In a small bowl, mix the coconut sugar, cinnamon, and cardamom well.
3. In the slow cooker, layer the bread, apples, and coconut sugar mixture.
4. In a large bowl, mix the eggs, coconut milk, apple juice, and vanilla, and mix well. Pour this mixture slowly over the food in the slow cooker. Sprinkle the granola on top.
5. Cover and cook on low for 4 to 5 hours, or until a food thermometer registers 165°F.
6. Scoop the mixture from the slow cooker to serve.

Vegetable Omelet

Prep time: 15 minutes | Cook time: 4 to 5 hours on low | Serves 8

- 1 tablespoon extra-virgin olive oil
- 10 eggs
- ½ cup heavy (whipping) cream
- 1 teaspoon minced garlic
- ¼ teaspoon salt
- ⅛ teaspoon freshly ground black pepper
- ½ cup chopped cauliflower
- ½ cup chopped broccoli
- 1 red bell pepper, chopped
- 1 scallion, white and green parts, chopped
- 4 ounces goat cheese, crumbled
- 2 tablespoons chopped parsley, for garnish

1. Lightly grease the insert of the slow cooker with the olive oil.
2. In a medium bowl, whisk together the eggs, heavy cream, garlic, salt, and pepper. Stir in the cauliflower, broccoli, red bell pepper, and scallion. Pour the mixture into the slow cooker. Sprinkle the top with goat cheese.
3. Cover and cook on low for 4 to 5 hours.
4. Serve topped with the parsley.

Sausage-Stuffed Peppers

Prep time: 15 minutes | Cook time: 4 to 5 hours on low | Serves 4

- 1 tablespoon extra-virgin olive oil
- 4 bell peppers, tops cut off and seeds removed
- 1 cup breakfast sausage (here), crumbled
- 6 eggs
- ½ cup coconut milk
- 1 scallion, white and green parts, chopped
- ½ teaspoon freshly ground black pepper
- 1 cup shredded cheddar cheese

1. Line a slow cooker insert with foil and grease the foil with the olive oil.
2. Place the four peppers in the slow cooker and evenly fill them with the sausage crumbles.
3. In a medium bowl, whisk together the eggs, coconut milk, scallion, and pepper. Pour the egg mixture into the four peppers. Next, sprinkle the cheese over them.
4. Cook on low for 4 to 5 hours, until the eggs are set.
5. Serve warm.

Cranberry-Ginger Compote

Prep time: 10 minutes | Cook time: 2 to 2 1/2 hours | Serves 4

- 1 chunk fresh ginger, about 5 inches long
- One 12-ounce bag fresh cranberries, rinsed and picked over for stems
- 1 cup sugar
- 1/4 cup water
- Grated zest and juice of 1 large orange
- 1/8 teaspoon ground cloves
- 1/2 cup walnuts, chopped
- 1/4 cup chopped crystallized ginger (optional)

1. Peel and coarsely grate the ginger. Take the grated ginger in your fist and squeeze out as much of the juice as you can into the slow cooker; discard the pulp.
2. Leave two-thirds of the cranberries whole and chop the rest. Add all the cranberries to the cooker, along with the sugar, water, orange zest and juice, and cloves. Cover and cook on HIGH for 2 to 2 1/2 hours; the whole cranberries will have popped open.
3. While still hot, stir in the walnuts and crystallized ginge. Scrape with a rubber spatula into clean spring-top glass jars (or use screw tops with new lids). Store, covered, in the refrigerator for up to 3 weeks. Serve chilled or at room temperature.

Apple-y Kielbasa

Prep time: 15 minutes | Cook time: 6-8 hours |
Serves 12

- 2 lbs. fully cooked kielbasa sausage, cut into 1-inch pieces
- ¾ cup brown sugar
- 1 cup chunky applesauce
- 2 cloves garlic, minced

1. Combine all ingredients in slow cooker.
2. Cover and cook on Low 6-8 hours until thoroughly heated.

Mexican Meat Dip

Prep time: 20 minutes | Cook time: ¾-1½ hours |
Serves 20

- 1 lb. ground beef
- ¾-1 cup chopped onions
- 15-oz. can refried beans
- 1 pkg. dry taco seasoning mix
- 1 cup sour cream
- 1½ cups shredded mozzarella cheese

1. Brown ground beef and onions in skillet.
2. Drain. Place meat and onions in slow cooker. Add beans and taco seasoning mix. Mix together well.
3. Spread sour cream over mixture. Sprinkle cheese over top.
4. Cover. Cook on Low 1½ hours, or on High ¾ hour.
5. Serve warm from the cooker with tortilla chips.

Mexican Ground Beef Cheese Dip

Prep time: 15 minutes | Cook time: 4-5 hours |
Serves 10

- 1 lb. ground beef
- 15-oz. can enchilada sauce
- 1 lb. Velveeta cheese, cubed

1. Brown ground beef in nonstick skillet. Drain.
2. Place in slow cooker. Add sauce and cubed cheese. Stir well.
3. Cover and cook on Low 4-5 hours.
4. When heated through, serve with your favorite taco chips.

Egg and Potato Strata

Prep time: 20 minutes | Cook time: 6-8 hours |
Serves 8

- 8 Yukon Gold potatoes, peeled and diced
- 1 onion, minced
- 2 red bell peppers, stemmed, seeded, and minced
- 3 Roma tomatoes, seeded and chopped
- 3 garlic cloves, minced
- 1½ cups shredded Swiss cheese
- 8 eggs
- 2 egg whites
- 1 teaspoon dried marjoram leaves
- 1 cup 2% milk

1. In a 6-quart slow cooker, layer the diced potatoes, onion, bell peppers, tomatoes, garlic, and cheese.
2. In a medium bowl, mix the eggs, egg whites, marjoram, and milk well with a wire whisk. Pour this mixture into the slow cooker.
3. Cover and cook on low for 6 to 8 hours, or until a food thermometer registers 165°F and the potatoes are tender.
4. Scoop out of the slow cooker to serve.

Quick and Easy Nacho Dip

Prep time: 15 minutes | Cook time: 2 hours |
Serves 10-15

- 1 lb. ground beef
- dash of salt
- dash of pepper
- dash of onion powder
- 2 garlic cloves, minced, optional
- 2 16-oz. jars salsa, your choice of heat
- 15-oz. can refried beans
- 1½ cups sour cream
- 3 cups shredded cheddar cheese, divided

1. Brown ground beef. Drain. Add salt, pepper, onion powder, and minced garlic.
2. Combine beef, salsa, beans, sour cream, and 2 cups cheese in slow cooker.
3. Cover. Heat on Low 2 hours. Just before serving sprinkle with 1 cup cheese.
4. Serve with tortilla chips.

Cranberry-Apple Chutney

Prep time: 10 minutes | Cook time: 4 1/2 to 5
hours | Serve 4

- 2 large shallots, peeled
- Zest of 1 large orange, cut off the fruit in strips with a small knife
- One 12-ounce bag fresh cranberries, rinsed and picked over for stems
- 2 large tart apples, such as Granny Smith, cored and finely chopped (you can peel or leave on the skin)
- 1 1/2 cups firmly packed dark brown sugar
- 1/2 cup dried currants or golden raisins or finely chopped dried apricots
- 1 chunk fresh ginger, about 1 inch long, peeled and grated
- 1/2 teaspoon curry powder
- 1/4 teaspoon ground cloves
- 1/4 teaspoon ground allspice
- 1/3 cup cider vinegar or raspberry vinegar
- 1/3 cup slivered almonds (2 ounces), toasted in a 325°F oven until pale gold, chopped

1. Coarsely chop the shallots and orange zest in a food processor.
2. Combine all the ingredients, except the almonds, in the slow cooker. Cover and cook on LOW for 4 to 4 1/2 hours, until the chutney achieves a jam-like consistency.
3. Remove the lid and let the chutney cook on LOW for an additional 30 minutes to evaporate excess juice and thicken, if necessary.
4. Stir in the almonds. Turn off the cooker and let the chutney cool in the slow cooker to room temperature. Scrape with a rubber spatula into clean spring-top glass jars (or use screw tops with new lids). Store, covered, in the refrigerator for up to 6 weeks. Serve chilled or at room temperature.

Mixed Berry Clafoutis

Prep time: 15 minutes | Cook time: 25 minutes | Serves 6

- 1 cup all-purpose flour
- 1¾ cups granulated sugar
- 1 teaspoon baking powder
- ¼ teaspoon salt
- ¼ teaspoon ground cinnamon
- ¼ teaspoon ground nutmeg
- 2 eggs, lightly beaten
- 3 teaspoons olive oil (extra-virgin)
- 2 tablespoons milk
- 2 cups fresh blueberries
- 2 cups fresh raspberries
- 2 cups fresh blackberries
- 1 cup water
- 3 tablespoons uncooked quick-cooking tapioca
- whipped cream, for serving

1. In a medium bowl, stir together the flour, ¾ cup of the sugar, baking powder, salt, cinnamon, and nutmeg.
2. In a small bowl, whisk together the eggs, olive oil, and milk.
3. Add the egg mixture to the flour mixture and stir to combine, just until moistened. Set aside.
4. In a large heavy saucepan over medium heat, combine the blueberries, raspberries, blackberries, the remaining 1 cup sugar, the water, and the tapioca. Bring to a boil.
5. Pour the hot fruit mixture into the slow cooker. Immediately spoon the batter over the fruit mixture.
6. Cover and cook on high for 1¾ to 2 hours or until a toothpick inserted into the center of the cake topper comes out clean.
7. Remove the crock from the cooker, if possible, or uncover and turn off the cooker. Let stand, uncovered, for 1 hour to cool slightly.
8. To serve, spoon the warm clafoutis into dessert dishes and top with the whipped cream.

Easy Barbecue Smokies

Prep time: 5 minutes | Cook time: 2 hours | Serves 12-16

- 18-oz. bottle barbecue sauce
- 8 ozs. salsa
- 2 16-oz. pkgs. little smokies

1. Mix barbecue sauce and salsa in slow cooker.
2. Add the little smokies.
3. Heat on High for 2 hours.
4. Stir. Turn to Low to serve.

Taco Pizza Dip

Prep time: 15 minutes | Cook time: 1½-2 hours | Serves 8-10

- 2 8-oz. pkgs. cream cheese, softened
- 8-12-oz. container French onion dip
- 1 lb. ground beef
- half an envelope dry taco seasoning mix
- 1 cup shredded cheddar cheese
- green pepper, diced, optional
- mushrooms, sliced, optional

1. Combine cream cheese and onion dip. Spread in slow cooker.
2. Brown ground beef in a skillet. Drain. Stir taco seasoning into meat.
3. Place seasoned meat on top of cream cheese mixture.
4. Sprinkle cheddar cheese on top of meat. Top with peppers and mushrooms, if you wish.
5. Cover and cook on Low 1½-2 hours. Serve with white corn chips.

Chapter 4

Breakfasts and Brunches

Vanilla Pumpkin Bread

Prep time: 10 minutes | Cook time: 2 hours |
Serves 2

- cooking spray
- ½ cup white flour
- ½ cup whole wheat flour
- ½ tsp baking soda
- A pinch of cinnamon powder
- 2 tbsp olive oil
- 2 tbsp maple syrup
- 1 egg
- ½ tbsp milk
- ½ tsp vanilla extract
- ½ cup pumpkin puree
- 2 tbsp walnuts, chopped
- 2 tbsp chocolate chips

1. In a bowl, mix white flour with whole wheat flour, baking soda and cinnamon and stir.
2. Add maple syrup, olive oil, egg, milk, vanilla extract, pumpkin puree, walnuts and chocolate chips and stir well.
3. Grease a loaf pan that fits your slow cooker with cooking spray, pour pumpkin bread, transfer to your cooker and cook on High for 2 hours.
4. Slice bread, divide between plates and serve.

Vanilla Barley Porridge

Prep time: 10 minutes | Cook time: 7 to 9 hours |
Serves 4

- 11/2 cups old-fashioned rolled barley flakes
- 2 tablespoons honey
- Pinch of salt
- 4 cups water
- 1 tablespoon unsalted butter
- 1/2 vanilla bean

For Serving:
- Sliced bananas
- Toasted almonds

1. Combine the barley, honey, salt, water, and butter in the slow cooker. Split the vanilla bean with the point of a small sharp knife; scrape out the seeds. Add the pod and seeds to the cooker and stir. Cover and cook on LOW for 7 to 9 hours, or overnight.
2. Remove the vanilla pod. Stir the cereal well and scoop into bowls with an oversized spoon. Serve with milk or cream and top with sliced bananas and toasted almonds.

Breakfast Casserole

Prep time: 15-20 minutes | Cook time: 12 hours |
Serves 8

- 4 cups daikon radish
- 12 oz cooked, crumbled bacon slices
- 1 lb. cooked grounded sausage
- 1 onion, chopped
- 1 green bell pepper, sliced
- 1 ½ cups mushroom, sliced
- 1 ½ cups fresh spinach
- 2 cups shredded cheese (Monterrey Jack is preferred)
- ½ cup feta cheese, shredded
- 10 eggs
- 1 cup heavy white cream

1. First of all, put a layer of hashed browns in the bottom of the cooker with low flame.
2. Then put the layer of bacon and sausage over it.
3. Put all the spices upon the layer.
4. Now take a bowl and whisk the eggs and cream and pour the mixture in the cooker.
5. Cover it and let it cook for 6 hours on high flame or for 12 hours on low flame.

Buttery Coconut Bread

Prep time: 10 minutes | Cook time: 3 to 4 hours on low | Makes 8 slices

- 1 tablespoon butter, softened
- 6 large eggs
- ½ cup coconut oil, melted
- 1 teaspoon pure vanilla extract
- ¼ teaspoon liquid stevia
- 1 cup almond flour
- ½ cup coconut flour
- 1 ounce protein powder
- 1 teaspoon baking powder

1. Grease an 8-by-4-inch loaf pan with the butter.
2. In a medium bowl, whisk together the eggs, oil, vanilla, and stevia until well blended.
3. In a small bowl, stir together the almond flour, coconut flour, protein powder, and baking powder until mixed.
4. Add the dry ingredients to the wet ingredients and stir to combine.
5. Spoon the batter into the loaf pan and place the loaf pan on a rack in the slow cooker.
6. Cover and cook on low for 3 to 4 hours, until a knife inserted in the center comes out clean.
7. Cool the bread in the loaf pan for 15 minutes. Then remove the bread from the pan and place onto a wire rack to cool completely.
8. Store in a sealed container in the refrigerator for up to 1 week.

Breakfast Skillet

Prep time: 15 minutes | Cook time: 2½-3 hours | Serves 4-5

- 3 cups milk
- 5½ oz. box au gratin potatoes
- 1 tsp. hot sauce
- 5 eggs, lightly beaten
- 1 tbsp. prepared mustard
- 4-oz. can sliced mushrooms
- 8 slices bacon, fried and crumbled
- 1 cup cheddar cheese, shredded

1. Combine milk, au gratin-sauce packet, hot sauce, eggs, and mustard.
2. Stir in dried potatoes, mushrooms, and bacon.
3. Cover. Cook on High 2½-3 hours, or on Low 5-6 hours.
4. Sprinkle cheese over top. Cover until melted.

Breakfast Sausage

Prep time: 10 minutes | Cook time: 3 hours on low | Serves 8

- 1 tablespoon extra-virgin olive oil
- 2 pounds ground pork
- 2 eggs
- 1 sweet onion, chopped
- ½ cup almond flour
- 2 teaspoons minced garlic
- 2 teaspoons dried oregano
- 1 teaspoon dried thyme
- ½ teaspoon salt

1. Lightly grease the insert of the slow cooker with the olive oil.
2. In a large bowl, stir together the pork, eggs, onion, almond flour, garlic, oregano, thyme, fennel seeds, pepper, and salt until well mixed.
3. Transfer the meat mixture to the slow cooker's insert and shape it into a loaf, leaving about ½ inch between the sides and meat.
4. Cover, and if your slow cooker has a temperature probe, insert it.
5. Cook on low until it reaches an internal temperature of 150°F, about 3 hours.
6. Slice in any way you prefer and serve.

Steamed Brown Bread

Prep time: 10 minutes | **Cook time:** 2 to 2 1/2 hours | **Serves 4**

- 1 large egg
- 1/2 cup sugar
- 1/2 cup light molasses
- 1 cup whole milk
- 1 cup whole wheat pastry flour
- 1 teaspoon baking soda
- 1/2 teaspoon salt
- 1/4 teaspoon ground nutmeg

1. Grease and flour a 1 1/2-quart (6-cup) pudding mold, heat-proof bowl, or small slow cooker that will fit inside your slow cooker with an inch or so of clearance all around.
2. In a medium-size bowl, beat the egg with a whisk. Add the sugar and molasses and continue to beat until thoroughly mixed. Beat in the milk. In a small bowl, whisk together the flour, baking soda, salt, and nutmeg, then add to the molasses mixture and stir just until the ingredients are thoroughly combined. Pour the batter into the prepared mold. Place the cover on the mold or, if you are using a bowl, cover it tightly with a double layer of aluminum foil; tie a string around the rim of the bowl to hold the foil in place.
3. Lower the mold into the slow cooker and carefully add enough hot water to come about 2 inches up the sides of the mold. Cover and cook on HIGH for 2 to 2 1/2 hours. To determine if the bread is done, carefully remove the lid or foil from the mold and gently touch the center of the bread. It should spring back into place. If your finger leaves an impression, re-cover the bread and cooker and continue to steam, checking the bread at 30-minute intervals.
4. When the bread is done, carefully transfer the mold to a rack and let the bread cool, uncovered, for 10 minutes. Run a table knife around the inside of the mold to loosen the bread. Invert onto a rack to remove the mold, then turn the bread right side up to cool. To serve, cut into wedges or slices.

Custom Hot Cereal Blends

Prep time: 10 minutes | **Cook time:** 1 hour | **Serves 5**

Hot Apple Granola
- 1 1/2 cups steel-cut oats
- 1 cup cracked wheat
- 1 cup cracked rye
- 1 cup barley grits
- 1 cup minced dried apples
- 3/4 cup dried currants
- 2 teaspoons ground cinnamon or apple pie spice

Four-Grain Cereal Flakes
- 1 cup old-fashioned or thick-cut rolled oats (not quick cooking)
- 1 cup rolled wheat
- 1 cup rye flakes
- 1 cup old-fashioned rolled barley flakes

Hot Apple Granola
1. In a large bowl, combine all the ingredients; mix well.
2. Store in a covered container or plastic bag at room temperature.
3. Use in any recipe calling for steel-cut oats.

Four-Grain Cereal Flakes
1. In a large bowl, combine all the ingredients; mix well.
2. Store in a covered container or plastic bag at room temperature.
3. Use in any recipe calling for rolled oats.

Rebecca's Rustic Whole Oat Porridge

Prep time: 10 minutes | Cook time: 7 to 9 hours | Serves 4

- 1 cup oat groats
- Pinch of fine sea salt
- One 4-inch cinnamon stick
- 4 1/4 cups water

1. Combine all the ingredients in the slow cooker. Cover and cook on LOW for 7 to 9 hours, or overnight. (If you have the time, set the cooker to HIGH for 1 to 2 hours to start the cooking; this is optional.)
2. Discard the cinnamon stick. Stir the porridge well and scoop into bowls with an oversized spoon.

Slow cooker-Baked Hominy Cornbread

Prep time: 10 minutes | Cook time: 2 1/4 to 2 1/2 hours | Serves 4

- 1 1/4 cups medium- or fine-grind yellow cornmeal, preferably stoneground
- 3/4 cup all-purpose flour
- 1/4 cup whole wheat pastry flour
- 2 tablespoons sugar
- 1 tablespoon baking powder
- 1 teaspoon salt
- 2 large eggs
- 3/4 cup canned golden or white hominy, rinsed and drained
- 1 cup whole milk
- 6 tablespoons (3/4 stick) unsalted butter or leaf lard, melted

For Serving:
- Butter
- Strawberry jam

1. Line the bottom of the slow cooker with a round of parchment paper. Coat the paper and the sides of the cooker, one-third of the way up, with butter-flavor nonstick cooking spray, or grease with butter.
2. Whisk together the cornmeal, flours, sugar, baking powder, and salt in a medium-size bowl. Make a well in the center and add the eggs, hominy, milk, and melted butter. with a large spoon or dough whisk, stir the dry ingredients into the liquid center until all the ingredients are moistened and thoroughly blended; take care not to overmix or break up the hominy too much. Spread the batter evenly in the cooker. Cover and cook on HIGH until a cake tester inserted into the center comes out clean, 2 1/4 to 2 1/2 hours.
3. Turn the cooker off, remove the lid, and let stand for 30 minutes to cool. To remove the cornbread, run a knife around the inside edge of the cooker and lift it out with a large rubber spatula. Cut into small wedges and serve warm with butter and jam.

Breakfast Bake

Prep time: 15 minutes | Cook time: 3-4 hours | Serves 10

- 12 eggs
- 1½-2 cups shredded cheese, your choice
- 1 cup diced cooked ham
- 1 cup milk
- 1 tsp. salt
- ½ tsp. pepper

1. Beat eggs. Pour into slow cooker.
2. Mix in remaining ingredients.
3. Cover and cook on Low 3-4 hours.

Huevos Rancheros

Prep time: 10 minutes | Cook time: 3 hours on low | Serves 8

- 1 tablespoon extra-virgin olive oil
- 10 eggs
- 1 cup heavy (whipping) cream
- 1 cup shredded monterey jack cheese, divided
- 1 cup prepared or homemade salsa
- 1 scallion, green and white parts, chopped
- 1 jalapeño pepper, chopped
- ½ teaspoon chili powder
- ½ teaspoon salt
- 1 avocado, chopped, for garnish
- 1 tablespoon chopped cilantro, for garnish

1. Lightly grease the insert of the slow cooker with the olive oil.
2. In a large bowl, whisk together the eggs, heavy cream, ½ cup of the cheese, salsa, scallion, jalapeño, chili powder, and salt. Pour the mixture into the insert and sprinkle the top with the remaining ½ cup of cheese.
3. Cover and cook until the eggs are firm, about 3 hours on low.
4. Let the eggs cool slightly, then cut into wedges and serve garnished with avocado and cilantro.

Steamed Winter Squash Bread

Prep time: 10 minutes | Cook time: 2 to 2 1/2 hours | Serves 4

- 1 large egg
- 1/2 cup honey
- 3/4 cup winter squash or pumpkin purée
- 1/2 cup whole wheat flour
- 1/2 cup all-purpose flour
- 1/3 cup fine- or medium-grind yellow cornmeal
- 1 teaspoon baking soda
- 1/2 teaspoon salt
- 1/4 cup chopped pitted dates
- 1/4 cup chopped walnuts

1. Grease and flour a 1 1/2-quart (6-cup) pudding mold, heat-proof bowl, or small slow cooker crock that will fit inside your slow cooker with an inch or so of clearance all around.
2. In a medium-size bowl, beat the egg and honey together with a wooden spoon, then beat in the squash. In a small bowl, whisk together the flours, cornmeal, baking soda, and salt. Add the dry ingredients to the squash mixture and stir just until thoroughly combined. Stir in the dates and walnuts. Pour the batter into the prepared mold. Place the cover on the mold or, if you are using a bowl, cover it tightly with a double layer of aluminum foil; tie a string around the rim of the bowl to hold the foil in place.
3. Lower the mold into the slow cooker and carefully add enough hot water to come about 2 inches up the sides of the mold. Cover and cook on HIGH for 2 hours. To determine if the bread is done, carefully remove the lid or foil and gently touch the center of the bread. It should spring back into place. If your finger leaves an impression, re-cover the bread and cooker and continue to steam, checking at 30-minute intervals.
4. When the bread is done, carefully transfer the mold to a rack and let cool, uncovered, for 10 minutes. Run a table knife around the inside of the mold to loosen the bread. Invert onto a rack to remove the mold, then turn the bread right side up to cool. Cut into wedges or slices and serve.

Hot Barley Breakfast Cereal

Prep time: 10 minutes | Cook time: 7 to 9 hours | Serves 4

- 2 cups old-fashioned rolled barley flakes
- Pinch of fine sea salt
- 4 1/2 cups water

1. Combine the ingredients in the slow cooker. Cover and cook on LOW for 7 to 9 hours, or overnight.
2. Stir the cereal well and scoop into bowls with an oversized spoon. Serve with milk or soy milk and maple syrup, honey, or brown sugar.

Sage Potato Casserole

Prep time: 10 minutes | Cook time: 3 hours and 30 minutes | Serves 2

- 1 tsp onion powder
- 3 eggs, whisked
- ½ tsp garlic powder
- ½ tsp sage, dried
- Salt and black pepper to the taste
- ½ yellow onion, chopped
- 1 tbsp parsley, chopped
- 2 garlic cloves, minced
- a pinch of red pepper flakes
- ½ tbsp olive oil
- 2 red potatoes, cubed

1. Grease your slow cooker with the oil, add potatoes, onion, garlic, parsley and pepper flakes and toss a bit.
2. In a bowl, mix eggs with onion powder, garlic powder, sage, salt and pepper, whisk well and pour over potatoes.
3. Cover, cook on High for 3 hours and 30 minutes, divide into 2 plates and serve for breakfast.

Creamy Rice Porridge with Raisins

Prep time: 10 minutes | Cook time: 6 to 8 hours | Serves 4

- 1 cup medium-grain rice, such as Calrose, or short-grain rice, such as Arborio
- 2 cups water
- 1 1/2 cups evaporated skim milk
- 1/2 teaspoon salt
- 1/2 cup raisins

1. Combine all the ingredients in the slow cooker. Cover and cook on LOW until tender and creamy, 6 to 8 hours or overnight.
2. Stir the porridge well and serve straight from the pot with no embellishment.

Western Omelet Casserole

Prep time: 15 minutes | Cook time: 8-9 hours | Serves 10

- 32-oz. bag frozen hash brown potatoes
- 1 lb. cooked ham, cubed
- 1 medium onion, diced
- 1½ cups shredded cheddar cheese
- 12 eggs
- 1 cup milk
- 1 tsp. salt
- 1 tsp. pepper

1. Layer one-third each of frozen potatoes, ham, onions, and cheese in bottom of slow cooker. Repeat 2 times.
2. Beat together eggs, milk, salt, and pepper.
3. Pour over mixture in slow cooker. Cover. Cook on Low 8-9 hours.
4. Serve with orange juice and fresh fruit.

Steamed Molasses Brown Bread

Prep time: 10 minutes | Cook time: 2 to 2 1/2 hours | Serves 4

- 1/3 cup light molasses
- 1 1/3 cups buttermilk
- 1/2 cup whole wheat flour
- 1/2 cup medium rye flour
- 1/2 cup medium- or fine-grind yellow cornmeal
- 1 1/4 teaspoons baking soda
- 1/2 teaspoon salt
- 1/3 cup raisins

1. Grease and flour a 1 1/2-quart (6-cup) pudding mold, heat-proof bowl, or small slow cooker crock that will fit inside your slow cooker with an inch or so of clearance all around.
2. In a medium-size bowl, beat together the molasses and buttermilk with a wooden spoon. In another medium-size bowl, whisk together the flours, cornmeal, baking soda, and salt. Add the dry ingredients to the molasses mixture and stir just until thoroughly combined. Stir in the raisins. Pour the batter into the prepared mold. Place the cover on the mold or, if you are using a bowl, cover it tightly with a double layer of aluminum foil; tie a string around the rim of the bowl to hold the foil in place.
3. Lower the mold into the slow cooker and carefully add enough hot water to come about 2 inches up the sides of the mold. Cover and cook on HIGH for 2 hours. To determine if the bread is done, carefully remove the lid or foil and gently touch the center of the bread. It should spring back into place. If your finger leaves an impression, re-cover the bread and cooker and continue to steam, checking at 30-minute intervals.
4. When the bread is done, carefully transfer the mold to a rack and let cool, uncovered, for 10 minutes. Run a table knife around the inside of the mold to loosen the bread. Invert onto a rack to remove the mold, then turn the bread right side up to cool. Cut into wedges or slices and serve.

Almond & Strawberry Oatmeal

Prep time: 10 minutes | Cook time: 6 hours | Serves 2

- 1 cup steel cut oats
- 3 cups water
- 1 cup almond milk
- 1 cup strawberries, chopped
- ½ cup Greek yogurt
- ½ tsp cinnamon powder
- ½ tsp vanilla extract

1. In your slow cooker, mix oats with water, milk, strawberries, yogurt, cinnamon and vanilla, toss, cover and cook on Low for 6 hours.
2. Stir your oatmeal one more time, divide into bowls and serve for breakfast.

Creamy Cornmeal Porridge

Prep time: 10 minutes | Cook time: 7 to 9 hours | Serves 4

- 1/2 cup coarse cornmeal, polenta, or corn grits, stone-ground if possible
- 2 cups water
- Pinch of salt
- 1/2 cup evaporated milk

1. Combine all the ingredients in the slow cooker. Cover and cook on LOW for 7 to 9 hours, or overnight. Stir a few times with a whisk or wooden spoon, if possible, during cooking.
2. Stir the porridge well and scoop into bowls with an oversized spoon. Serve with a pat of butter, milk, and a sprinkle of toasted wheat germ; or stir in cream cheese or mascarpone and top with berries.

Bacon-Mushroom Breakfast

Prep time: 15 minutes | Cook time: 4 hours | Serves 4

- 3½ oz bacon large, sliced
- 2½ oz white mushrooms, chopped
- 5 eggs
- ¼ cup shallots, chopped
- ¾ cup bell pepper, chopped
- 6 kale leaves large, shredded
- 1 cup Parmesan cheese

1. Clean the kale leaves, remove the hard stems and chop into small pieces.
2. In a skillet cook the bacon, till it becomes crispy and add mushrooms, red pepper, and shallot.
3. Add kale and cut down the flame and let the kale become tender in the skillet.
4. Now take a medium bowl and beat all eggs.
5. In the slow cooker, add ghee and let it become hot.
6. Spread the ghee on all side of the cooker.
7. Put the sautéed vegetable into the base of the cooker.
8. Spread the cheese over the vegetables.
9. Then, add the beaten eggs on top.
10. Just stir it gently.
11. Set the cooker on low heat and cook for about 4 hours.
12. Serve hot with sliced avocado(optional).

Cheddar Sausage Potatoes

Prep time: 10 minutes | Cook time: 4 hours | Serves 2

- 2 potatoes, chopped
- ½ red bell pepper, chopped
- ½ green bell pepper, chopped
- ½ yellow onion, chopped
- 4 oz smoked Italian sausage, sliced
- 1 cup cheddar cheese, shredded
- ¼ cup sour cream
- A pinch of oregano, dried
- ¼ tsp basil, dried
- 4 oz chicken cream
- 1 tbsp parsley, chopped

1. Put the potato in your slow cooker, add red bell pepper, green bell pepper, onion, sausage, cheese, sour cream, oregano, basil, and chicken cream, cover and cook on Low for 4 hours.
2. Add parsley, toss, divide between plates and serve for breakfast.

Chapter 5

Poultry

Onion Turkey Breast

Prep time: 5 minutes | Cook time: 8-10 hours | Serves 6-8

- 4-6-lb. boneless, skinless turkey breast
- 1 tsp. garlic powder
- 1 envelope dry onion soup mix

1. Place turkey in slow cooker. Sprinkle garlic powder and onion soup mix over breast.
2. Cover. Cook on Low 8-10 hours.

Apricot Stuffing and Chicken

Prep time: 10 minutes | Cook time: 2-3½ hours | Serves 5

- 1 stick (8 tbsp.) butter, divided
- 1 box cornbread stuffing mix
- 4 boneless, skinless chicken breast halves
- 6-8-oz. jar apricot preserves

1. In a mixing bowl, make stuffing, using ½ stick (4 tbsp.) butter and amount of water called for in instructions on box. Set aside.
2. Cut up chicken into 1-inch pieces. Place on bottom of slow cooker. Spoon stuffing over top.
3. In microwave, or on stovetop, melt remaining ½ stick (4 tbsp.) butter with preserves. Pour over stuffing.
4. Cover and cook on High for 2 hours, or on Low for 3½ hours, or until chicken is tender but not dry.

Filipino Chicken Adobo

Prep time: 10 minutes | Cook time: 3 to 3 1/2 hours | Serves 4

- 3/4 cup plain rice vinegar
- 1/2 cup low-sodium soy sauce
- 4 cloves garlic, pressed
- One 2- to 3-inch piece fresh ginger, peeled and grated (optional)
- 1 tablespoon light brown sugar
- 1 teaspoon black peppercorns
- 2 bay leaves
- 2 1/2 pounds bone-in, skin-on chicken thighs (about 8), trimmed of fat
- 1 pound red or Yukon gold potatoes, scrubbed and cut into eights
- 2 medium-size carrots, sliced, or 2 cups baby carrots
- 4 ounces green beans, ends trimmed
- 2 tablespoons olive oil
- 3/4 cup water

1. In a shallow glass baking dish, stir together the vinegar, soy sauce, garlic, ginger (if using), brown sugar, peppercorns, and bay leaves. Add the chicken and turn to coat. Cover and marinate in the refrigerator for at least 1 hour or as long as overnight.
2. Place the potatoes, carrots, and green beans in the slow cooker. Lift the chicken out of the marinade and pat dry with paper towels. Heat the oil in a large skillet over medium-high heat and cook the chicken, skin side down, until it is a golden brown on both sides, about 2 minutes per side. Transfer the chicken thighs to the slow cooker. Pour the marinade and water into the skillet and bring to a boil. Pour the sauce into the slow cooker.
3. Cover and cook on HIGH for 3 to 3 1/2 hours, or until the juice of the chicken runs clear. Discard the bay leaves. Serve the chicken and vegetables with the sauce.

Butter Chicken

Prep time: 20 minutes | Cook time: 7½–9½ hours | Serves 8

- ½ cup plain Greek yogurt
- ⅓ cup lemon juice
- 5 teaspoons curry powder
- 2 tablespoons grated fresh ginger root
- 10 4-ounce boneless, skinless chicken thighs
- 4 large tomatoes, seeded and chopped
- 2 onions, chopped
- 8 garlic cloves, sliced
- ⅔ cup canned coconut milk
- 3 tablespoons cornstarch

1. In a medium bowl, mix the yogurt, lemon juice, curry powder, and ginger root. Add the chicken and stir to coat; let stand for 15 minutes while you prepare the other ingredients.
2. In a 6-quart slow cooker, mix the tomatoes, onions, and garlic.
3. Add the chicken-yogurt mixture to the slow cooker. Cover and cook on low for 7 to 9 hours, or until the chicken registers 165°F on a food thermometer.
4. In a small bowl, mix the coconut milk and cornstarch. Stir into the slow cooker.
5. Cover and cook on low for another 15 to 20 minutes, or until the sauce has thickened.

Chicken in Mushroom Sauce

Prep time: 10–15 minutes | Cook time: 4–5 hours | Serves 4

- 4 boneless, skinless chicken breast halves
- 10¾-oz. can cream of mushroom soup
- 1 cup sour cream
- 7-oz. can mushroom stems and pieces, drained, optional
- 4 bacon strips, cooked and crumbled, or ¼ cup pre-cooked bacon crumbles
1. Place chicken in slow cooker.

2. In a mixing bowl, combine soup and sour cream, and mushroom pieces if you wish. Pour over chicken.
3. Cover and cook on Low 4–5 hours, or until chicken is tender, but not dry.
4. Sprinkle with bacon before serving.
5. Serve over cooked rice or pasta.

Butter & Herb Turkey

Prep time: 10 minutes | Cook time: 5 hours | Serves 12

- 1 bone-in turkey breast (6 to 7 pounds)
- 2 tablespoons butter, softened
- $\frac{1}{2}$ teaspoon dried rosemary, crushed
- $\frac{1}{2}$ teaspoon dried thyme
- $\frac{1}{4}$ teaspoon garlic powder
- $\frac{1}{4}$ teaspoon pepper
- 1 can (14 $\frac{1}{2}$ ounces) chicken broth
- 3 tablespoons cornstarch
- 2 tablespoons cold water

1. Rub turkey with butter. Combine the rosemary, thyme, garlic powder and pepper; sprinkle over turkey. Place in a 6-qt. slow cooker. Pour broth over top. Cover and cook on low for 5–6 hours or until tender.
2. Remove turkey to a serving platter; keep warm. Skim fat from cooking juices; transfer to a small saucepan. Bring to a boil.
3. Combine cornstarch and water until smooth. Gradually stir into the pan. Bring to a boil; cook and stir for 2 minutes or until thickened. Serve with the turkey.

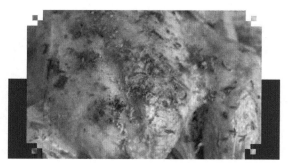

Apple Balsamic Chicken

Prep time: 15 minutes | Cook time: 4 hours | Serves 4

- 4 bone-in chicken thighs (about 1 ¹/₂ pounds), skin removed
- ¹/₂ cup chicken broth
- ¹/₄ cup apple cider or juice
- ¹/₄ cup balsamic vinegar
- 2 tablespoons lemon juice
- ¹/₂ teaspoon salt
- ¹/₂ teaspoon garlic powder
- ¹/₂ teaspoon dried thyme
- ¹/₂ teaspoon paprika
- ¹/₂ teaspoon pepper
- 2 tablespoons butter
- 2 tablespoons all-purpose flour

1. Place chicken in a 1¹/₂-qt. slow cooker. In a small bowl, combine the broth, cider, vinegar, lemon juice and seasonings; pour over meat. Cover and cook on low for 4-5 hours or until chicken is tender.
2. Remove chicken; keep warm. Skim fat from cooking liquid. In a small saucepan, melt butter; stir in flour until smooth. Gradually add cooking liquid. Bring to a boil; cook and stir for 2-3 minutes or until thickened. Serve with chicken.

Sesame Chicken Wings

Prep time: 35-40 minutes | Cook time: 2½-5 hours | Makes 6-8 main-dish , or 16 appetizers

- 3 lbs. chicken wings
- salt to taste
- pepper to taste
- 1¾ cups honey
- 1 cup soy sauce
- ½ cup ketchup
- 2 tbsp. canola oil
- 2 tbsp. sesame oil
- 2 garlic cloves, minced
- toasted sesame seeds

1. Rinse wings. Cut at joint. Sprinkle with salt and pepper. Place on broiler pan.
2. Broil 5 inches from top, 10 minutes on each side. Place chicken in slow cooker.
3. Add remaining ingredients except sesame seeds. Pour over chicken.
4. Cover. Cook on Low 5 hours, or on High 2½ hours.
5. Sprinkle sesame seeds over top just before serving.
6. Serve as appetizer, or with white or brown rice and shredded lettuce to turn this appetizer into a meal.

Salsa Chicken

Prep time: 10 minutes | Cook time: 3 to 3 ¹/2 hours | Serves 4

- 6 boneless, skinless chicken breast halves (about 2 pounds), trimmed of fat
- 1 1/2 cups thick prepared salsa of your choice, medium or hot
- 1 teaspoon ground cumin
- Pinch of pure ground red chile powder
- 3 tablespoons fresh lime juice

1. Coat the slow cooker with nonstick cooking spray and arrange the chicken in it. Pour the salsa over the chicken. Cover and cook on HIGH until the chicken is tender and cooked through, 3 to 3 1/2 hours. The chicken will make some of its own juice, thinning out the salsa a bit.
2. Stir in the cumin, chile powder, and lime juice, cover, and cook for another 15 minutes before serving.

Easy Mushroom Chicken

Prep time: 5-10 minutes | Cook time: 3-8 hours | Serves 4-6

- 4-6 chicken legs and thighs (joined), skinned
- salt and pepper to taste
- ½ cup chicken broth or dry white wine
- 10¾-oz. can cream of mushroom or celery soup
- 4-oz. can sliced mushrooms, drained

1. Sprinkle salt and pepper on each piece of chicken. Place chicken in slow cooker.
2. In a small bowl, mix broth and soup together. Pour over chicken.
3. Spoon mushrooms over top.
4. Cover and cook on Low 6-8 hours, or on High 3-4 hours, or until chicken is tender but not dry.

Chicken with Beer

Prep time: 10 minutes | Cook time: 3 to 4 hours | Serves 4

- About 3/4 cup all-purpose flour
- 4 boneless chicken breast halves, with skin on
- 2 tablespoons unsalted butter
- 1/2 cup beer
- 1 teaspoon salt
- 1/8 teaspoon freshly ground black pepper
- 1/4 teaspoon dried herbes de Provence
- 2 bay leaves, broken in half

1. Put the flour on a shallow plate or a pie plate. One piece at a time, dredge the chicken in the flour, coating both sides and shaking off any excess.
2. Melt the butter in a large skillet over medium-high heat. When it foams, add the chicken, skin side down, and cook until deep golden brown on both sides, 5 to 7 minutes per side. Transfer the chicken to the slow cooker. Add the beer to the skillet and bring it to a boil, scraping up any browned bits stuck to the pan. Pour over the chicken. Sprinkle with the salt, pepper, and herbes de Provence. Tuck the bay leaves in among the chicken pieces. Cover and cook on HIGH for 3 to 4 hours.
3. Preheat the oven to 400°F. with a slotted spoon, transfer the chicken to a shallow baking dish. Discard the bay leaves. Pour any liquid remaining in the cooker over the chicken. Bake, uncovered, until lightly browned, about 20 minutes. Serve immediately.

Chili Barbecued Chicken Wings

Prep time: 5 minutes | Cook time: 2-8 hours | Makes 10 main-dish

- 5 lbs. chicken wings, tips cut off
- 12-oz. bottle chili sauce
- ⅓ cup lemon juice
- 1 tbsp. Worcestershire sauce
- 2 tbsp. molasses
- 1 tsp. salt
- 2 tsp. chili powder
- ¼ tsp. hot pepper sauce
- dash garlic powder

1. Place wings in cooker.
2. Combine remaining ingredients and pour over chicken.
3. Cover. Cook on Low 6-8 hours, or on High 2-3 hours.

One-Dish Chicken Supper

Prep time: 5 minutes | Cook time: 6-8 hours |
Serves 4

- 4 boneless, skinless chicken breast halves
- 10¾-oz. can cream of chicken or celery or mushroom soup
- ⅓ cup milk
- 1 pkg. Stove Top stuffing mix and seasoning packet
- 1⅔ cups water

1. Place chicken in slow cooker.
2. Combine soup and milk. Pour over chicken.
3. Combine stuffing mix, seasoning packet, and water. Spoon over chicken.
4. Cover. Cook on Low 6-8 hours.

Miso Chicken

Prep time: 20 minutes | Cook time: 7-8 hours |
Serves 8

- 1 onion, chopped
- 3 garlic cloves, minced
- 2 tablespoons grated fresh ginger root
- 2 pounds skinless chicken drumsticks
- 2 pounds skinless chicken thighs
- 2 cups Chicken Stock , divided
- 2 tablespoons honey
- 2 tablespoons miso paste
- 2 tablespoons toasted sesame seeds
- 4 scallions, cut on the bias

1. In a 6-quart slow cooker, mix the onion, garlic, and ginger root. Top with the chicken drumsticks and thighs.
2. In a medium bowl, mix ½ cup of the chicken stock with the honey and miso paste and whisk to blend. Add the remaining 1½ cups of the chicken stock and mix until well blended, then pour this mixture into the slow cooker.

3. Cover and cook on low for 7 to 8 hours, or until the chicken registers 165°F on a food thermometer.
4. Sprinkle with the sesame seeds and scallions and serve.

Teriyaki Chicken Thighs

Prep time: 10 minutes | Cook time: 5 1/2 to 6
hours | Serves 4

- 12 bone-in chicken thighs
- 1 tablespoon vegetable oil
- 1/2 cup sake
- 1/4 cup mirin
- 2 tablespoons soy sauce
- 2 teaspoons light or dark brown sugar

1. Remove the skin from the thighs. Trim away and discard any large pieces of fat. Heat the oil in a large, heavy skillet over high heat. A cast-iron skillet is ideal. When hot, add the chicken in a single layer, in batches, without crowding, smooth side (formerly the skin side) down. Cook until deep golden brown on both sides, 3 to 4 minutes per side. As they brown, transfer the thighs to the slow cooker. Pour off any fat from the skillet. Add the sake, mirin, soy sauce, and brown sugar to the skillet, bring to a boil, and cook, scraping up any browned bits stuck to the pan. Pour over the chicken. Cover and cook on HIGH until the chicken is cooked through and beginning to brown, 4 1/2 to 5 hours.
2. Use a spoon or turkey baster to pour some of the sauce over the chicken. Leave the lid off and cook 1 hour more on HIGH, until the chicken has browned and the sauce has reduced by about half.
3. Place the chicken on a platter and pour the sauce remaining in the cooker over it.

Easy Turkey Breast

Prep time: 5 minutes | Cook time: 6-7 hours |
Serves 12

- 1 Jenny O'Turkey Breast—with bone in and with gravy packet
- salt

1. Wash frozen breast and sprinkle with salt.
2. Place turkey, gravy packet up, in slow cooker that's large enough to be covered when the turkey breast is in it.
3. Cover. Cook turkey on Low 6-7 hours, or until tender, removing gravy packet when the turkey is partially thawed. (Keep packet in refrigerator.)
4. Make gravy according to directions on packet. Warm before serving.

Creamy Nutmeg Chicken

Prep time: 25 minutes | Cook time: 3 hours |
Serves 6

- 6 boneless chicken breast halves
- oil
- ¼ cup chopped onions
- ¼ cup minced parsley
- 2 10¾-oz. cans cream of mushroom soup
- ½ cup sour cream
- ½ cup milk
- 1 tbsp. ground nutmeg
- ¼ tsp. sage
- ¼ tsp. dried thyme
- ¼ tsp. crushed rosemary

1. Brown chicken in skillet in oil. Reserve drippings and place chicken in slow cooker.
2. Sauté onions and parsley in drippings until onions are tender.
3. Stir in remaining ingredients. Mix well. Pour over chicken.
4. Cover. Cook on Low 3 hours, or until

juices run clear.

5. Serve over mashed or fried potatoes, or rice.

Five-Spice Chicken Wings

Prep time: 30 minutes | Cook time: 2½-5½ hours
| Serves 6-8

- 3 lbs. (about 16) chicken wings
- 1 cup bottled plum sauce (check an Asian grocery, or the Asian food aisle in a general grocery store)
- 2 tbsp. butter, melted
- 1 tsp. five-spice powder (check an Asian grocery, or the Asian food aisle in a general grocery store)
- thinly sliced orange wedges, optional
- pineapple slices, optional

1. In a foil-lined baking pan arrange the wings in a single layer. Bake at 375° for 20 minutes. Drain well.
2. Meanwhile, combine the plum sauce, melted butter, and five-spice powder in your slow cooker. Add wings. Then stir to coat the wings with sauce.
3. Cover and cook on Low 4-5 hours, or on High 2-2½ hours.
4. Serve immediately, or keep them warm in your slow cooker on Low for up to 2 hours.
5. Garnish with orange wedges and pineapple slices to serve, if you wish.

Caribbean Jerked Chicken

Prep time: 10 minutes | Cook time: 5 to 6 hours | Serves 4

- 1/2 cup sliced green onions (white part and some of the green; about 12)
- 2 tablespoons grated fresh ginger
- 1 1/2 teaspoons ground allspice
- 1/2 teaspoon ground cinnamon
- 1 tablespoon olive oil
- 3 jalapeños, seeded and coarsely chopped
- 1 teaspoon freshly ground black pepper
- 1/2 teaspoon salt
- Pinch of red pepper flakes
- 1 to 2 cloves garlic, to your taste, pressed
- 2 tablespoons firmly packed dark brown sugar
- 1 tablespoon cider vinegar
- 1 tablespoon orange juice
- 2 teaspoons Worcestershire sauce
- 4 bone-in chicken thighs, with skin on, and 4 drumsticks

1. In a food processor, combine the green onions, ginger, allspice, cinnamon, oil, jalapeños, black pepper, salt, red pepper flakes, and garlic and process until very finely chopped, almost smooth. Stir in the brown sugar, vinegar, orange juice, and Worcestershire to form a paste. Using a brush, apply the jerk sauce so it completely coats the chicken; use up all of the sauce.
2. Put a wire rack in the slow cooker. Place the chicken on the rack. Cover and cook on LOW until the chicken is tender and cooked through, 5 to 6 hours. Serve immediately.

Turkey Breast with Orange Sauce

Prep time: 15-20 minutes | Cook time: 7-8 hours | Serves 4-6

- 1 large onion, chopped
- 3 garlic cloves, minced
- 1 tsp. dried rosemary
- ½ tsp. pepper
- 2-3-lb. boneless, skinless turkey breast
- 1½ cups orange juice

1. Place onions in slow cooker.
2. Combine garlic, rosemary, and pepper.
3. Make gashes in turkey, about ¾ of the way through at 2-inch intervals. Stuff with herb mixture. Place turkey in slow cooker.
4. Pour juice over turkey.
5. Cover. Cook on Low 7-8 hours, or until turkey is no longer pink in center.

Lemony Turkey Breast

Prep time: 10 minutes | Cook time: 5-7 hours | Serves 12

- 1 5-lb. bone-in turkey breast, cut in half and skin removed, partially frozen in center
- 1 medium lemon, halved
- 1 tsp. lemon-pepper seasoning
- 1 tsp. garlic salt
- 4 tsp. cornstarch
- ½ cup fat-free, reduced-sodium chicken broth

1. Place turkey, meaty side up, in slow cooker sprayed with non-fat cooking spray.
2. Squeeze half of lemon over turkey. Sprinkle with lemon pepper and garlic salt.
3. Place lemon halves under turkey.
4. Cover. Cook on Low 5-7 hours.
5. Remove turkey. Discard lemons.
6. Allow turkey to rest 15 minutes before slicing.

Chapter 6

Beef, Pork and Lamb

Pork Chops on Rice

Prep time: 30 minutes | Cook time: 4-9 hours | Serves 4

- ½ cup brown rice
- ⅔ cup converted white rice
- ¼ cup butter
- ½ cup chopped onions
- 4-oz. can sliced mushrooms, drained
- ½ tsp. dried thyme
- ½ tsp. sage
- ½ tsp. salt
- ¼ tsp. black pepper
- 4 boneless pork chops, ¾-1-inch thick
- 10½-oz. can beef consomme
- 2 tbsp. Worcestershire sauce
- ½ tsp. dried thyme
- ½ tsp. paprika
- ¼ tsp. ground nutmeg

1. Sauté white and brown rice in butter in skillet until rice is golden brown.
2. Remove from heat and stir in onions, mushrooms, thyme, sage, salt, and pepper. Pour into greased slow cooker.
3. Arrange chops over rice.
4. Combine consomme and Worcestershire sauce. Pour over chops.
5. Combine thyme, paprika, and nutmeg. Sprinkle over chops.
6. Cover. Cook on Low 7-9 hours, or on High 4-5 hours.

Chuck Wagon Beef

Prep time: 20 minutes | Cook time: 8¼-10¼ hours | Serves 8

- 4-lb. boneless chuck roast
- 1 tsp. garlic salt
- ¼ tsp. black pepper
- 2 tbsp. oil
- 6-8 garlic cloves, minced
- 1 large onion, sliced
- 1 cup water
- 1 bouillon cube
- 2-3 tsp. instant coffee
- 1 bay leaf, or 1 tbsp. mixed Italian herbs
- 3 tbsp. cold water
- 2 tbsp. cornstarch

1. Sprinkle roast with garlic salt and pepper. Brown on all sides in oil in saucepan. Place in slow cooker.
2. Sauté garlic and onion in meat drippings in saucepan. Add water, bouillon cube, and coffee. Cook over low heat for several minutes, stirring until drippings loosen. Pour over meat in cooker.
3. Add bay leaf or herbs.
4. Cover. Cook on Low 8-10 hours, or until very tender. Remove bay leaf and discard. Remove meat to serving platter and keep warm.
5. Mix water and cornstarch together until paste forms. Stir into hot liquid and onions in cooker. Cover. Cook 10 minutes on High, or until thickened.
6. Slice meat and serve with gravy over top or on the side.

Beef Ribs with Sauerkraut

Prep time: 10 minutes | Cook time: 3-8 hours | Serves 8-10

- 3-4 lbs. beef short ribs
- 32-oz. bag or 27-oz. can sauerkraut, drained
- 2 tbsp. caraway seeds
- ¼ cup water

1. Put ribs in 6-quart slow cooker.
2. Place sauerkraut and caraway seeds on top of ribs.
3. Pour in water.
4. Cover. Cook on High 3-4 hours, or on Low 7-8 hours.
5. Serve with mashed potatoes.

Lamb Goulash Au Blanc

Prep time: 10 minutes | Cook time: 5 to 6 hours | Serves 4

- 3 tablespoons unsalted butter, softened
- 1 medium-size yellow onion, chopped
- 2 pounds fresh spring lamb stew meat, such as shoulder, cut into 1 1/2-inch cubes
- 1 lemon, seeded and very thinly sliced
- 1 teaspoon caraway seeds
- 2 teaspoons dried marjoram
- 1 clove garlic, peeled
- 1 cup vegetable broth
- Salt and freshly ground black pepper to taste

1. Smear the bottom of the slow cooker with the butter and sprinkle with the onion. Put the lamb in the cooker, and arrange the lemon slices over it.
2. In a mortar, mash together the caraway seeds, marjoram, and garlic with a pestle; stir into the broth. Add the broth to the cooker, cover, and cook on LOW until the lamb is fork-tender, 5 to 6 hours. Season with salt and pepper and serve.

Mississippi Beef Roast

Prep time: 10 minutes |Cook time: 6 to 8 hours| Serves 8

- 1½ tablespoons extra-virgin olive oil
- 1 (3- to 4-pound) boneless chuck roast
- 1¼ teaspoons kosher salt
- 1½ teaspoons freshly ground black pepper
- ¼ cup all-purpose flour
- 4 tablespoons (½ stick) unsalted butter
- 10 pepperoncini
- 2 tablespoons mayonnaise
- 1 tablespoon sour cream
- 2 teaspoons apple cider vinegar
- 1 teaspoon buttermilk
- ½ teaspoon dried dill
- ½ teaspoon dried chives

1. In a slow cooker with a stove-top function, or in a Dutch oven or heavy-bottomed pan over medium-high heat, heat the oil until shimmering. Season the roast with the specified amount of salt and pepper, and coat with the flour. Brown the roast on both sides to create a crust, about 4 minutes per side.
2. Place the roast in the slow cooker, along with the butter, pepperoncini, mayonnaise, sour cream, cider vinegar, buttermilk, dill, and chives. Cover and cook on low for 6 to 8 hours, until tender.
3. Transfer the meat to a cutting board. Using two forks, shred the meat and discard any fat. Return the meat to the slow cooker and mix the meat with the liquid inside, or plate the meat and drizzle the tangy au jus on top.

Savory Mexican Pot Roast

Prep time: 15 minutes | Cook time: 10-12 hours | Serves 6-8

- 3 lbs. beef brisket, cubed
- 2 tbsp. oil
- ½ cup slivered almonds
- 2 cups mild picante sauce, or hot, if you prefer
- 2 tbsp. vinegar
- 1 tsp. garlic powder
- ½ tsp. salt
- ¼ tsp. cinnamon
- ¼ tsp. dried thyme
- ¼ tsp. dried oregano
- ⅛ tsp. ground cloves
- ⅛ tsp. pepper
- ½-¾ cup water, as needed

1. Brown beef in oil in skillet. Place in slow cooker.
2. Combine remaining ingredients. Pour over meat.
3. Cover. Cook on Low 10-12 hours. Add water as needed.

Chicago-Style Italian Beef

Prep time: 15 minutes | Cook time: 4 hours | Serves 6

- 3 pounds thinly sliced deli-style Italian beef
- 2 large onions, thinly sliced
- 2 red bell peppers, seeded and sliced
- 6 garlic cloves, very thinly sliced
- 1 tablespoon smoked sweet paprika or Hungarian paprika
- 1 teaspoon kosher salt
- 1 teaspoon cayenne pepper
- 1 teaspoon dried oregano
- ½ teaspoon freshly ground black pepper
- 1½ cups Beef Bone Broth (here) or low-sodium if store-bought
- 1 cup dry red wine
- 3 tablespoons Worcestershire sauce
- Loaf of French bread, for the sandwich
- Jar of hot giardiniera, for garnish

1. In the slow cooker, place the deli meat, onions, bell peppers, garlic, paprika, salt, cayenne, oregano, pepper, bone broth, wine, and Worcestershire sauce. Stir to combine. Cover and cook on low for 4 hours.
2. Slice the French bread and, for each sandwich, tuck some Italian Beef between two pieces of bread. Top with some of the cooking liquid and a few pieces of bell pepper. Serve with the giardiniera.

Apples, Sauerkraut, and Chops

Prep time: 25 minutes | Cook time: 4-8 hours | Serves 4

- 4 pork chops, ½-inch thick, browned
- 1 onion, sliced and separated into rings
- ⅛ tsp. garlic flakes or powder
- 3 cups sauerkraut, drained
- 1 cup unpeeled apple slices
- 1½ tsp. caraway seeds

- ¼ tsp. salt
- ¼ tsp. dried thyme
- ¼ tsp. pepper
- ¾ cup apple juice

1. Place half of onions, garlic flakes, sauerkraut, apple slices, and caraway seeds in slow cooker. Season with half the salt, thyme, and pepper.
2. Add pork chops.
3. Layer remaining ingredients in order given.
4. Pour apple juice over all.
5. Cover. Cook on Low 6-8 hours, or on High 4 hours.

Apple-Cranberry Pork Roast

Prep time: 20 minutes | Cook time: 6-8 hours | Serves 8

- 2 lbs. pork tenderloin, fat trimmed
- 2 tbsp. canola oil
- 3 cups apple juice
- 3 Granny Smith apples
- 1 cup fresh cranberries
- ¾ tsp. salt
- ½ tsp. black pepper

1. Brown roast on all sides in skillet in canola oil. Place in slow cooker.
2. Add remaining ingredients.
3. Cover. Cook on Low 6-8 hours.

Braised Lamb Chops with White Beans

Prep time: 10 minutes | Cook time: 5 to 7 hours | Serves 4

- 1 to 2 tablespoons olive oil, as needed
- 4 shoulder lamb chops
- 1 medium-size yellow onion, chopped
- 1/2 cup chicken broth
- 1/2 cup dry white wine
- 1/4 cup chopped oil-packed sun-dried tomatoes, drained
- 1/2 teaspoon dried marjoram or thyme
- Pinch of ground cumin
- One 15-ounce can small white beans, rinsed and drained
- Salt and freshly ground black pepper to taste
- Hot cooked rice for serving

1. In a large nonstick skillet, heat the oil and brown the lamb on both sides over medium-high heat; transfer to the slow cooker. Add the onion to the skillet and cook for a few minutes until limp; add to the cooker. Add the broth, wine, tomatoes, marjoram, and cumin, cover, and cook on LOW for 2 1/2 to 3 1/2 hours.
2. Add the beans, cover, and continue to cook on LOW until the lamb is very tender, another 2 1/2 to 3 1/2 hours. Season with salt and pepper and serve over rice.

Sweet Pepper Steak

Prep time: 30 minutes | Cook time: 6 1/4 hours | Serves 12

- 1 beef top round roast (3 pounds)
- 1 large onion, halved and sliced
- 1 large green pepper, cut into $1/2$-inch strips
- 1 large sweet red pepper, cut into $1/2$-inch strips
- 1 cup water
- 4 garlic cloves, minced
- $1/3$ cup cornstarch
- $1/2$ cup reduced-sodium soy sauce
- 2 teaspoons sugar
- 2 teaspoons ground ginger
- 8 cups hot cooked brown rice

1. Place roast, onion and peppers in a 5-qt. slow cooker. Add water and garlic. Cook, covered, on low 6-8 hours or until meat is tender.
2. Remove beef to a cutting board. Transfer vegetables and cooking juices to a large saucepan. Bring to a boil. In a small bowl, mix cornstarch, soy sauce, sugar and ginger until smooth; stir into vegetable mixture. Return to a boil, stirring constantly; cook and stir 1-2 minutes or until thickened.
3. Cut beef into slices. Stir gently into sauce; heat through. Serve with rice.

Short Ribs In Red Wine

Prep time: 30 minutes | Cook time: 6 ¼ hours | Serves 6

- 3 pounds bone-in beef short ribs
- ½ teaspoon salt
- ½ teaspoon pepper
- 1 tablespoon canola oil
- 4 medium carrots, cut into 1-inch pieces
- 1 cup beef broth
- 4 fresh thyme sprigs
- 1 bay leaf
- 2 large onions, cut into ½-inch wedges
- 6 garlic cloves, minced
- 1 tablespoon tomato paste
- 2 cups dry red wine or beef broth
- 4 teaspoons cornstarch
- 3 tablespoons cold water
- Salt and pepper to taste

1. Sprinkle ribs with ½ teaspoon each salt and pepper. In a large skillet, heat oil over medium heat. In batches, brown ribs on all sides; transfer to a 4- or 5-qt. slow cooker. Add carrots, broth, thyme and bay leaf to ribs.
2. Add onions to the same skillet; cook and stir over medium heat 8-9 minutes or until tender. Add garlic and tomato paste; cook and stir 1 minute longer. Stir in the wine. Bring to a boil; cook 8-10 minutes or until liquid is reduced by half. Add to the slow cooker. Cook, covered, on low 6-8 hours or until meat is tender.
3. Remove ribs and vegetables; keep warm. Transfer cooking juices to a small saucepan; skim fat. Discard thyme and bay leaf. Bring juices to a boil. In a small bowl, mix cornstarch and water until smooth; stir into cooking juices. Return to a boil; cook and stir 1-2 minutes or until thickened. Season with salt and pepper to taste. Serve with ribs and vegetables.

Pork Tenderloin and Sauerkraut

Prep time: 10 minutes | Cook time: 8 to 10 hours | Serves 4

- 2 tablespoons olive oil
- 2 pounds pork tenderloin, trimmed of silver skin and fat, and blotted dry
- 4 small yellow onions, quartered
- 6 cloves garlic, minced
- 6 medium-size red potatoes, cut in half
- 8 grinds of black pepper
- One 1-pound bag fresh sauerkraut, rinsed

1. In a large skillet over medium-high heat, heat the oil until very hot. Add the meat and cook until browned on all sides, 4 to 5 minutes total. Transfer to the slow cooker. Tuck the onions around the tenderloin, then sprinkle with the garlic and top with the potato halves. Sprinkle with the pepper, and cover with the sauerkraut. Cover and cook on LOW until the pork is fork-tender, 8 to 10 hours.
2. Transfer the pork and vegetables to a platter. Slice the tenderloin into thick portions, and arrange on dinner plates, surrounded with some of each vegetable and some sauerkraut.

Beef Bourguignon

Prep time: 25 minutes |Cook time: 8 hours|
Serves 6

- 1 tablespoon extra-virgin olive oil
- 3 pounds beef stew meat
- 3 thick-cut bacon slices, finely chopped
- 3 tablespoons all-purpose flour
- 1 cup fruity red wine
- 2 tablespoons cognac or brandy
- 1 pound fresh mushrooms, sliced
- 3 carrots, peeled and sliced on the bias
- 18 pearl onions, peeled
- 2 garlic cloves, smashed
- 2 cups Beef Bone Broth (here) or low-sodium if store-bought
- 2 bay leaves
- ¾ teaspoon kosher salt, plus more for seasoning
- ½ teaspoon freshly ground black pepper, plus more for seasoning
- 1½ tablespoons cornstarch
- 1½ tablespoons cold water

1. In a slow cooker with a stove-top function, or in a Dutch oven or heavy-bottomed pan over medium-high heat, heat the oil until shimmering. In a large bowl, gently toss the beef and bacon with salt, pepper, and the flour, and brown, about 4 minutes per side. Add the wine and cognac, then raise the heat to high and deglaze the pan, scraping the brown bits from the bottom.
2. If browned, transfer the meat and bacon to a plate. Line the bottom of the slow cooker with the mushrooms. Place the meat and bacon on top of the mushrooms. Add the carrots, pearl onions, and garlic.
3. If you skipped browning, whisk the flour into the bone broth until no lumps remain. Add it to the slow cooker with the bay leaves, salt, and pepper. Cover and cook on low for 8 hours.
4. About 30 minutes before serving, whisk together the cornstarch and water in a small bowl. Add to the slow cooker and gently stir. Leave the lid slightly ajar and continue cooking until the cooking liquid has thickened and the meat is tender. Discard the bay leaves. Using a ladle or large spoon, skim the fat from the top of the liquid or refrigerate for a couple of hours until the fat solidifies and can be spooned off. Season with additional salt and pepper, as needed.

Pork Chops with Stuffing

Prep time: 15 minutes | Cook time: 4-5 hours |
Makes 2

- 4 slices bread, cubed
- 1 egg
- ¼ cup grated or finely chopped celery
- ¼-½ tsp. salt
- ⅛ tsp. pepper
- 2 thickly cut pork chops
- 1 cup water

1. Combine bread cubes, eggs, celery, salt, and pepper.
2. Cut pork chops part way through, creating a pocket. Fill with stuffing.
3. Pour water into slow cooker. Add chops.
4. Cover. Cook on Low 4-5 hours.

Lamb Curry

Prep time: 10 minutes | Cook time: 6 to 8 hours | Serves 4

- 2 to 4 tablespoons cooking oil
- 2 medium-size yellow onions, chopped
- 2 pounds shoulder of lamb, shank, or butt roast, trimmed of visible fat and cut into 2-inch cubes
- One 1/2-inch piece fresh ginger, peeled
- 2 cloves garlic, peeled
- 2 serrano or jalapeño chiles, seeded
- 1 cup vegetable or chicken broth
- 1 tablespoon ground cumin
- 1 tablespoon ground coriander
- 1/2 teaspoon ground turmeric
- 1 1/2 tablespoons all-purpose flour
- One 14-ounce can unsweetened coconut milk
- 2 large tart apples, such as Fuji or Granny Smith, peeled, cored, and coarsely chopped
- 5 green cardamom pods
- 3 black cardamom pods
- One 4-inch cinnamon stick
- 1 bay leaf
- 4 cloves
- 1 teaspoon salt, or to taste
- 1/2 cup plain yogurt
- 1/3 cup fruit chutney, processed until smooth in a food processor

For Serving:
- Hot cooked basmati rice
- 1/2 cup chopped fresh cilantro

1. In a large nonstick skillet, heat half the oil over medium-high heat and brown half the onions and lamb on all sides, about 10 minutes. Remove them to the cooker and brown the remaining onions and lamb. Add to the cooker.
2. Chop the ginger, garlic, and chiles together in a mini food processor and add a bit of the broth to make a paste.

Add this to the skillet along with the cumin, coriander, and turmeric and cook, stirring constantly, for a few minutes. Sprinkle with the flour and add the remaining broth; stir until smooth, then pour into the cooker and add the coconut milk and apples. Put the cardamom pods, cinnamon stick, bay leaf, and cloves in a cheesecloth bag; nestle into the mixture. Cover and cook on HIGH for 1 hour.
3. Turn the cooker to LOW and cook until the lamb is very tender, 6 to 8 hours.
4. Discard the spice bag and season the curry with the salt. Stir in the yogurt and chutney; let sit, covered, in the cooker for 15 minutes to heat. Serve with basmati rice garnished with the cilantro.

Fruity Corned Beef and Cabbage

Prep time: 10 minutes | Cook time: 5-12 hours | Serves 6

- 2 medium onions, sliced
- 2½-3-lb. corned beef brisket
- 1 cup apple juice
- ¼ cup brown sugar, packed
- 2 tsp. finely shredded orange peel
- 6 whole cloves
- 2 tsp. prepared mustard
- 6 cabbage wedges

1. Place onions in slow cooker. Place beef on top of onions.
2. Combine apple juice, brown sugar, orange peel, cloves, and mustard. Pour over meat.
3. Place cabbage on top.
4. Cover. Cook on Low 10-12 hours, or on High 5-6 hours.

Louisiana Round Steak

**Prep time: 20 minutes | Cook time: 7 hours |
Serves 6**

- 2 pounds sweet potatoes, peeled and cut into 1-inch pieces
- 1 large onion, chopped
- 1 medium green pepper, sliced
- 2 beef top round steaks ($^3/_4$ inch thick and 1 pound each)
- 1 teaspoon salt, divided
- 2 tablespoons olive oil
- 1 garlic clove, minced
- 3 tablespoons all-purpose flour
- 1 can (28 ounces) diced tomatoes, undrained
- $^1/_2$ cup beef broth
- 1 teaspoon sugar
- $^1/_2$ teaspoon dried thyme
- $^1/_2$ teaspoon pepper
- 1/4 teaspoon hot pepper sauce

1. Place the sweet potatoes, onion and green pepper in a 6-qt. slow cooker. Cut each steak into three serving-size pieces; sprinkle with $^1/_2$ teaspoon salt. In a large skillet over medium heat, brown steaks in oil in batches on both sides. Place steaks over vegetables, reserving drippings in pan.
2. Add garlic to drippings; cook and stir for 1 minute. Stir in flour until blended. Stir in the remaining ingredients and remaining salt. Bring to a boil, stirring constantly. Cook and stir for 4–5 minutes or until thickened. Pour over meat. Cover and cook on low for 7–9 hours or until beef is tender.

Corned Beef and Cabbage

Prep time: 10 minutes |Cook time: 8 hours| Serves 8

- 1 (4 pound) flat-cut corned beef brisket, trimmed of excess fat

- 2 tablespoons pickling spice
- 4 large carrots, peeled and cut into large chunks
- 1 large onion, thinly sliced
- 2 garlic cloves, thinly sliced
- 10 small red potatoes, halved
- 4 cups water
- 6 ounces beer
- 1 small head green cabbage, cored and roughly chopped
- 2 tablespoons unsalted butter

1. Put the meat in the slow cooker, along with the pickling spice, carrots, onion, garlic, and potatoes. Pour the water and beer on top. Cover and cook on low for 8 hours.
2. About 1 hour before serving, add the cabbage to the slow cooker. Cover and continue to cook. When the meat and vegetables are done, discard the cooking liquid. To serve, thinly slice the meat against the grain and serve with the vegetables. Be sure to pass the butter for melting on top of the cabbage.

Meatballs In Tomato-Wine Sauce

Prep time: 10 minutes | Cook time: high to start, then 5 to 6 hours | Serves 4

Sauce:
- 2 tablespoons olive oil
- 1 large yellow onion, finely chopped
- 2 to 3 cloves garlic, to your taste, minced
- 3/4 cup dry red wine
- One 28-ounce can diced tomatoes, with their juice; or one 28-ounce can tomato purée
- One 6-ounce can tomato paste
- 1 teaspoon salt
- 1/2 teaspoon freshly ground black pepper
- 1 teaspoon dried basil or 1 tablespoon minced fresh basil
- 1 teaspoon dried oregano or 1 tablespoon minced fresh oregano
- 1/4 teaspoon ground allspice
- 1 bay leaf
- 2 tablespoons minced fresh flat-leaf parsley, or more to taste

Meatballs:
- 1 1/2 pounds lean ground beef
- 1 cup plain dry bread crumbs
- 2 large eggs
- 3 tablespoons freshly grated Parmesan cheese
- 1 teaspoon salt
- 1/4 teaspoon freshly ground black pepper
- 1/4 teaspoon dried basil or 3/4 teaspoon minced fresh basil
- 1/4 teaspoon dried oregano or 3/4 teaspoon minced fresh oregano
- 1/4 cup minced fresh flat-leaf parsley
- Dash of ground allspice
- 1 1/2 tablespoons olive oil
- 1/4 cup dry red wine

1. To prepare the sauce, heat the olive oil in a large nonstick skillet over medium-high heat. Add the onion and garlic and cook, stirring a few times, until softened but not browned, about 5 minutes. Add the wine, bring to a boil, and continue boiling for 1 to 2 minutes, scraping up any browned bits stuck to the bottom of the pan.

2. Transfer to the slow cooker. Add the tomatoes, tomato paste, salt, pepper, basil, oregano, parsley, allspice, and bay leaf and stir to combine. Cover and cook on HIGH while you prepare the meatballs.

3. To prepare the meatballs, put the ground beef in a large bowl, breaking it up a bit with your fingers or a large fork. Add the bread crumbs, eggs, Parmesan, salt, pepper, basil, oregano, parsley, and allspice. Gently but thoroughly blend the ingredients, using your hands or a large fork. Be careful not to compact the meat, which will make your meatballs tough. Gently shape the mixture into 12 meatballs, each a bit bigger than a golf ball.

4. Heat the olive oil in a large nonstick skillet over medium-high heat. Add the meatballs and brown on all sides, turning carefully, 6 to 10 minutes total. Using a slotted spoon, transfer them to the sauce. Pour off any fat from the skillet, return to the stove, and add the wine. Cook over high heat for 2 or 3 minutes, scraping up any browned bits stuck to the pan. Pour over the meatballs. If the meatballs are not covered by tomato sauce, carefully spoon some sauce over them. Cover and cook on LOW for 5 to 6 hours. Remove the bay leaf and serve the meatballs and sauce over pasta.

Mahogany Glazed Pork

Prep time: 10 minutes | Cook time: 8 to 10 hours | Serves 4

- 1/3 cup soy sauce
- 1/2 cup orange marmalade
- 1 to 2 cloves garlic, to your taste, pressed
- 1 to 1 1/2 teaspoons red pepper flakes, to your taste
- 3 tablespoons ketchup
- One 3 1/2-pound boneless Boston pork butt, cut into large pieces, or 3 1/2 pounds country-style pork spareribs
- 8 ounces sugar snap peas
- 1/2 cup julienned red bell pepper

1. Coat the slow cooker with nonstick cooking spray.
2. Combine the soy sauce, marmalade, garlic, red pepper flakes, and ketchup in a small bowl and mix until smooth; brush over both sides of the meat. Arrange the pork butt or ribs in the cooker. (If you have a round cooker, stack the ribs.) Pour over any extra sauce. Cover and cook on LOW until fork-tender and the meat starts to separate from the bone, 8 to 10 hours.
3. Stir in the sugar snap peas and bell pepper; cover and let stand a few minutes to warm. Serve immediately.

Cabbage and Corned Beef

Prep time: 15 minutes | Cook time: 5-10 hours | Serves 12

- 3 large carrots, cut into chunks
- 1 cup chopped celery
- 1 tsp. salt
- ½ tsp. black pepper
- 1 cup water
- 4-lb. corned beef
- 1 large onion, cut into pieces
- 4 potatoes, peeled and chunked
- half a small head of cabbage, cut in wedges

1. Place carrots, celery, seasonings, and water in slow cooker.
2. Add beef. Cover with onions.
3. Cover. Cook on Low 8-10 hours, or on High 5-6 hours. (If your schedule allows, this dish has especially good taste and texture if you begin it on High for 1 hour, and then turn it to Low for 5-6 hours, before going on to Step 4.)
4. Lift corned beef out of cooker and add potatoes, pushing them to bottom of slow cooker. Return beef to cooker.
5. Cover. Cook on Low 1 hour.
6. Lift corned beef out of cooker and add cabbage, pushing the wedges down into the broth. Return beef to cooker.
7. Cover. Cook on Low 1 more hour.
8. Remove corned beef. Cool and slice on the diagonal. Serve surrounded by vegetables.

Autumn Harvest Pork Loin

Prep time: 30 minutes | Cook time: 5-6 hours | Serves 4-6

- 1 cup cider or apple juice
- 1½-2-lb. pork loin
- salt
- pepper
- 2 large Granny Smith apples, peeled and sliced
- 1½ whole butternut squashes, peeled and cubed
- ½ cup brown sugar
- ¼ tsp. cinnamon
- ¼ tsp. dried thyme
- ¼ tsp. dried sage

1. Heat cider in hot skillet. Sear pork loin on all sides in cider.
2. Sprinkle meat with salt and pepper on all sides. Place in slow cooker, along with juices.
3. Combine apples and squash. Sprinkle with sugar and herbs. Stir. Place around pork loin.
4. Cover. Cook on Low 5-6 hours.
5. Remove pork from cooker. Let stand 10-15 minutes. Slice into ½-inch-thick slices.
6. Serve topped with apples and squash.

Zesty Beef Brisket Sliders

Prep time: 10 minutes |Cook time: 8 hours| Serves 12

- 1½ tablespoons extra-virgin olive oil
- 1 (3-pound) flat-cut beef brisket, trimmed of excess fat
- 2 pounds small potatoes, scrubbed and left whole
- 3 carrots, peeled and cut into chunks
- 1 medium onion, minced
- 2 (14.5-ounce) cans fire-roasted, diced tomatoes
- 1 tablespoon brown sugar
- ¼ cup dry red wine
- 1½ tablespoons balsamic vinegar
- 1 tablespoon Worcestershire sauce
- 1 teaspoon kosher salt
- ½ teaspoon freshly ground black pepper
- 12 soft slider rolls, sliced
- 1 large red onion, sliced

1. In a slow cooker with a stove-top function, or in a Dutch oven or heavy-bottomed pan over medium-high heat, heat the oil until shimmering. Season the brisket with salt and pepper, and brown, about 4 minutes per side.
2. Put the brisket in the slow cooker, along with the potatoes, carrots, onion, tomatoes, brown sugar, wine, vinegar, Worcestershire sauce, salt, and pepper. Stir to combine. Cover and cook on low for 8 to 10 hours, or until tender. Remove the cover, taste, and adjust the seasonings, as needed.
3. Transfer the brisket to a cutting board and let it rest for 10 minutes. Slice the meat against the grain. Remove the vegetables from the slow cooker and reserve them for another use.
4. Divide the meat evenly into 12 servings and tuck the brisket into each roll. Spoon the sauce on top of the sliders. and add 1 or 2 slices of red onion per slider.

Chapter 7

Fish and Seafood

Coconut Curry Shrimp

Prep time: 15 minutes | Cook time: 2 hours & 30 minutes | Serves 4

- 1 lb. wild-caught shrimp, peeled and deveined
- 2 ½ tsp lemon garlic seasoning
- 2 tbsp red curry paste
- 4 tbsp chopped cilantro
- 30 oz coconut milk, unsweetened
- 16 oz of water

1. Whisk together all the ingredients except for shrimps and 2 tbsp cilantro and add to a 4-quart slow cooker.
2. Plugin the slow cooker, shut with lid, and cook for 2 hours at high heat setting or 4 hours at low heat setting.
3. Then add shrimps, toss until evenly coated and cook for 20 to 30 minutes at high heat settings or until shrimps are pink.
4. Garnish shrimps with remaining cilantro and serve.

Shrimp and Artichoke Barley Risotto

Prep time: 15 minutes | Cook time: 25 minutes | Serves 4

- 3 cups seafood stock (or chicken stock)
- 1 teaspoon olive oil
- 1 yellow onion, chopped
- 3 cloves garlic, minced
- one 9-ounce package frozen artichoke hearts, thawed and quartered
- 1 cup uncooked pearl barley
- black pepper
- 1 pound shrimp, peeled and deveined
- 2 ounces parmesan or pecorino romano cheese, grated
- 2 teaspoons lemon zest
- 4 ounces fresh baby spinach

1. Bring the stock to a boil in a medium saucepan. Remove from the heat and set aside.
2. In a nonstick medium skillet over medium-high heat, heat the olive oil. Add the onion and sauté until tender, about 5 minutes. Add the garlic and sauté for 1 more minute.
3. Transfer the onion and garlic to the slow cooker and add the artichoke hearts and barley. Season with some pepper. Stir in the seafood stock.
4. Cover and cook on high for 3 hours, or until the barley is tender and the liquid is just about all absorbed.
5. About 15 minutes before the cooking time is completed, stir in the shrimp and grated cheese. Cover and continue to cook on high for another 10 minutes, or until the shrimp are opaque.
6. Add the lemon zest and fold in the baby spinach, stirring until it's wilted, about 1 minute.
7. Divide the risotto among the serving bowls and serve hot.

Crumb-Topped Haddock

Prep time: 5 minutes | Cook time: 35 minutes |
Serves 6

- 2 pounds haddock or cod fillets
- 1 can (10 $^3/_4$ ounces) condensed cream of shrimp soup, undiluted
- 1 teaspoon grated onion
- 1 teaspoon Worcestershire sauce
- 1 cup crushed butter-flavored crackers (about 25 crackers)

1. Preheat oven to 375°. Arrange fillets in a greased 13x9-in. baking dish. Combine soup, onion and Worcestershire sauce; pour over fish.
2. Bake, uncovered, 20 minutes. Sprinkle with cracker crumbs. Bake 15 minutes longer or until fish flakes easily with a fork.

Shrimp with Marinara Sauce

Prep time: 15 minutes | Cook time: 25 minutes |
Serves 4

- one 15-ounce can diced tomatoes, with the juice one
- 6-ounce can tomato paste
- 1 clove garlic, minced
- 2 tablespoons minced fresh flat-leaf parsley
- ½ teaspoon dried basil
- 1 teaspoon dried oregano
- 1 teaspoon garlic powder
- 1½ teaspoons sea salt
- ¼ teaspoon black pepper
- 1 pound cooked shrimp, peeled and deveined
- 2 cups hot cooked spaghetti or linguine, for serving
- ½ cup grated parmesan cheese, for serving

1. Combine the tomatoes, tomato paste, and minced garlic in the slow cooker. Sprinkle with the parsley, basil, oregano, garlic powder, salt, and pepper.
2. Cover and cook on low for 6 to 7 hours.
3. Turn up the heat to high, stir in the cooked shrimp, and cover and cook on high for about 15 minutes longer.
4. Serve hot over the cooked pasta. Top with Parmesan cheese.

Tuna Barbecue

Prep time: 10 minutes | Cook time: 4-10 hours |
Serves 4

- 12-oz. can tuna, drained
- 2 cups tomato juice
- 1 medium green pepper, finely chopped
- 2 tbsp. onion flakes
- 2 tbsp. Worcestershire sauce
- 3 tbsp. vinegar
- 2 tbsp. sugar
- 1 tbsp. prepared mustard
- 1 rib celery, chopped
- dash chili powder
- ½ tsp. cinnamon
- dash of hot sauce, optional

1. Combine all ingredients in slow cooker.
2. Cover. Cook on Low 8-10 hours, or on High 4-5 hours. If mixture becomes too dry while cooking, add ½ cup tomato juice.
3. Serve on buns.

Fettuccine with Smoked Salmon

Prep time: 10 minutes | Cook time: 1 to 2 hours | Serves 4

- 2 cups heavy cream
- 3 to 4 ounces top quality lox or smoked salmon, chopped or flaked into 1/2-inch pieces
- 1 pound fresh fettuccine, regular egg or spinach flavored
- 2 tablespoons olive oil (optional)
- Freshly ground black pepper to taste

1. Combine the cream and the lox in the slow cooker. Cover and cook on LOW until very hot, 1 to 2 hours.
2. Meanwhile, cook the fettuccine in boiling water until tender to the bite, about 3 minutes. Take care not to overcook. Toss with the olive oil if the pasta is to stand for over 5 minutes.
3. Add the fettuccine to the hot sauce and toss to coat evenly. If your cooker is large enough, just add the pasta to the cooker; if not, pour the sauce over the pasta in a shallow, heated bowl. Garnish with a few grinds of black pepper and serve immediately.

Creole Crayfish

Prep time: 15 minutes | Cook time: 25 minutes | Serves 2

- 1½ cups diced celery
- 1 large yellow onion, chopped
- 2 small bell peppers, any colors, chopped
- 1 8-ounce can tomato sauce
- 1 28-ounce can whole tomatoes, broken up, with the juice
- 1 clove garlic, minced
- 1 teaspoon sea salt
- ¼ teaspoon black pepper
- 6 drops hot pepper sauce (like tabasco)

- 1 pound precooked crayfish meat

1. Place the celery, onion, and bell peppers in the slow cooker. Add the tomato sauce, tomatoes, and garlic. Sprinkle with the salt and pepper and add the hot sauce.
2. Cover and cook on high for 3 to 4 hours or on low for 6 to 8 hours.
3. About 30 minutes before the cooking time is completed, add the crayfish.
4. Serve hot.

Company Seafood Pasta

Prep time: 15 minutes | Cook time: 1-2 hours | Serves 4-6

- 2 cups sour cream
- 3 cups shredded Monterey Jack cheese
- 2 tbsp. butter, melted
- ½ lb. crabmeat or imitation flaked crabmeat
- ⅛ tsp. pepper
- ½ lb. bay scallops, lightly cooked
- 1 lb. medium shrimp, cooked and peeled

1. Combine sour cream, cheese, and butter in slow cooker.
2. Stir in remaining ingredients.
3. Cover. Cook on Low 1-2 hours.
4. Serve immediately over linguine. Garnish with fresh parsley.

Macaroni Tuna Casserole

Prep time: 15 minutes | Cook time: 20 minutes | Serves 4

- 1 package (7 $\frac{1}{4}$ ounces) macaroni and cheese
- 1 can (10 $\frac{3}{4}$ ounces) condensed cream of celery soup, undiluted
- 1 can (5 ounces) tuna, drained and flaked
- $\frac{1}{2}$ cup milk
- 1 cup (4 ounces) shredded cheddar cheese
- Minced fresh parsley, optional

1. Preheat oven to 350°. Prepare macaroni and cheese according to package directions. Stir in soup, tuna and milk.
2. Pour into a greased 2-qt. baking dish. Sprinkle with cheese and, if desired, parsley.
3. Bake, uncovered, 20-25 minutes or until cheese is melted.

Salmon and Barley Bake

Prep time: 20 minutes | Cook time: 7½-8½ hours | Serves 6

- 2 cups hulled barley, rinsed
- 2 fennel bulbs, cored and chopped
- 2 red bell peppers, stemmed, seeded, and chopped
- 4 garlic cloves, minced
- 1 8-ounce package cremini mushrooms, sliced
- 5 cups Roasted Vegetable Broth
- 1 teaspoon dried tarragon leaves
- ⅛ teaspoon freshly ground black pepper
- 6 5-ounce salmon fillets
- ⅓ cup grated Parmesan cheese

1. In a 6-quart slow cooker, mix the barley, fennel, bell peppers, garlic, mushrooms, vegetable broth, tarragon, and pepper. Cover and cook on low for 7 to 8 hours, or until the barley has absorbed most of the liquid and is tender, and the vegetables are tender too.
2. Place the salmon fillets on top of the barley mixture. Cover and cook on low for 20 to 40 minutes longer, or until the salmon flakes when tested with a fork.
3. Stir in the Parmesan cheese, breaking up the salmon, and serve.

Cheesy Tuna-Stuffed Potatoes

Prep time: 10 minutes | Cook time: 3 ¾ to 6 hour | Serves 4

- 4 medium-size Idaho or russet potatoes, scrubbed and left dripping wet
- 3/4 cup finely shredded cheddar cheese
- 1/4 cup milk
- One 6-ounce can water-packed tuna, drained
- 1/2 cup sour cream (reduced fat is okay)
- 1 green onion (white and some of the green), thinly sliced

1. Prick each dripping-wet potato with a fork or the tip of a sharp knife and pile them into the slow cooker; do not add water. Cover and cook until fork-tender, on HIGH for 3 to 5 hours or on LOW for 6 to 8 hours.
2. Remove the potatoes from the cooker with tongs and cut in half lengthwise. Scoop out the center of Return to the slow cooker, setting down the stuffed potatoes in a single layer if possible so that they touch each other. Sprinkle with the remaining 1/4 cup of cheese. Cover and cook on HIGH for 45 minutes to 1 hour. Remove carefully from the cooker and serve immediately.

Citrus Sea Bass

Prep time: 10 minutes | Cook time: 1 1/2 hours | Serves 4

- 1 1/2 pounds sea bass fillets, rinsed and blotted dry
- Sea salt and white pepper to taste
- 1 medium-size white onion, chopped
- 1/4 cup minced fresh flat-leaf parsley
- 1 tablespoon grated lemon, lime, or orange zest or a combination
- 3 tablespoons dry white wine or water
- 1 tablespoon olive oil or toasted sesame oil

For Serving:
- Lemon wedges
- Lime wedges
- Cold tartar sauce

1. Coat the slow cooker with nonstick cooking spray or butter and arrange the fish in the crock. Season lightly with salt and white pepper, then add the onion, parsley, and zest. Drizzle with the wine and oil. Cover and cook on HIGH for 1 1/2 hours.
2. Carefully lift the fish out of the cooker with a plastic spatula or pancake turner. Serve immediately with lemon and lime wedges and tartar sauce.

Crab Zucchini Casserole

Prep time: 20 minutes | Cook time: 5 hours | Serves 2

- 1/4 cup heavy cream
- 2 zucchini squash
- 2 oz cream cheese
- 4 oz crab meat
- 1 tsp butter

1. Spiralize zucchini squash on wide ribbons and season with salt.
2. Place the ribbons in a steamer basket and heat for 5 to 7 minutes.
3. Put all ingredients in a slow cooker, including seasonings such as garlic, onions, pepper, and salt to taste.
4. Put the zucchini spirals on top—Cook within 5 hours on low.

Tuna Salad Casserole

Prep time: 10 minutes | Cook time: 5-8 hours | Serves 4

- 2 7-oz. cans tuna
- 10¾-oz. can cream of celery soup
- 3 hard-boiled eggs, chopped
- ½ to 1½ cups diced celery
- ½ cup diced onions
- ½ cup mayonnaise
- ¼ tsp. ground pepper
- 1½ cups crushed potato chips

1. Combine all ingredients except ¼ cup potato chips in slow cooker. Top with remaining chips.
2. Cover. Cook on Low 5-8 hours.

Chapter 8

Rice, Grains, and Beans

Easy Wheatberries

Prep time: 10 minutes | Cook time: 2 hours |
Serves 4-6

- 1 cup wheatberries
- 1 cup couscous or small pasta like orzo
- 14½-oz. can broth
- ½-1 broth can of water
- ½ cup dried craisins or raisins

1. Cover wheatberries with water and soak 2 hours before cooking. Drain. Spoon wheatberries into slow cooker.
2. Combine with remaining ingredients in slow cooker.
3. Cover. Cook on Low until liquid is absorbed and berries are soft, about 2 hours.

Gingery Quinoa Chicken

Prep time: 10 minutes | Cook time: 6 to 8 hours |
Serves 4

- 1 teaspoon extra-virgin olive oil
- ½ cup quinoa
- ½ cup low-sodium chicken broth
- ½ cup coconut milk
- 1 teaspoon minced fresh ginger
- 1 teaspoon minced garlic
- zest of 1 lime
- ½ teaspoon ground coriander
- 2 bone-in, skinless chicken thighs
- ⅛ teaspoon sea salt
- freshly ground black pepper
- juice of 1 lime, for garnish

1. Grease the inside of the slow cooker with the olive oil.
2. Put the quinoa, broth, coconut milk, ginger, garlic, zest, and coriander in the crock. Stir thoroughly.
3. Season the chicken thighs with the salt and a few grinds of the black pepper. Place them on top of the quinoa.

4. Cover and cook for 6 to 8 hours, until the quinoa has absorbed all the liquid and the chicken is cooked through.
5. Drizzle each portion with lime juice just before serving.

Slow Cooker Spaghetti Sauce

Prep time: 15 minutes | Cook time: 7 hours |
Serves 6-8

- 1 lb. ground beef
- 1 medium onion, chopped
- 2 14-oz. cans diced tomatoes, with juice
- 6-oz. can tomato paste
- 8-oz. can tomato sauce
- 1 bay leaf
- 4 garlic cloves, minced
- 2 tsp. dried oregano
- 1 tsp. salt
- 2 tsp. dried basil
- 1 tbsp. brown sugar
- ½-1 tsp. dried thyme

1. Brown meat and onion in saucepan. Drain well. Transfer to slow cooker.
2. Add remaining ingredients.
3. Cover. Cook on Low 7 hours. If the sauce seems too runny, remove lid during last hour of cooking.

Boston Baked Beans

Prep time: 10 minutes | Cook time: 1 1/2 hours | Serves 4

- 1 pound dried small white navy or pea beans
- 1/2 teaspoon baking soda
- One 8-ounce piece salt pork
- 1/2 cup dark molasses
- 1/2 cup firmly packed light or dark brown sugar
- 1 1/2 teaspoons dry mustard
- 1 1/2 teaspoons salt
- 1/4 teaspoon freshly ground black pepper
- 1 medium-size white onion, peeled, left whole, and scored with a crisscross through the root end
- 6 cups boiling water

1. Rinse the beans in a colander under cold running water and pick over for damaged beans and small stones. Transfer to the slow cooker. Cover with cold water by 2 inches, soak overnight, and then drain.
2. Cover the beans with fresh water by 3 inches. Add the baking soda, cover, and cook on HIGH until still undercooked, about 1 1/2 hours. Drain.
3. Meanwhile, simmer the salt pork in boiling water for 10 minutes to remove excess salt; drain and rinse under cold running water. Pat dry and dice.
4. Combine the drained beans, salt pork, molasses, brown sugar, mustard, salt, and pepper in the cooker; stir to mix well. Push the onion into the center of the beans and add the boiling water; it will cover everything by 1/2 inch. he beans are cooked with the cover off for the last 30 minutes to thicken them to the desired consistency.

Herbed Garlic Black Beans

Prep time: 10 minutes | Cook time: 7-9 hours | Serves 8

- 3 cups dried black beans, rinsed and drained
- 2 onions, chopped
- 8 garlic cloves, minced
- 6 cups low-sodium vegetable broth
- ½ teaspoon salt
- 1 teaspoon dried basil leaves
- ½ teaspoon dried thyme leaves
- ½ teaspoon dried oregano leaves

1. In a 6-quart slow cooker, mix all the ingredients. Cover and cook on low for 7 to 9 hours, or until the beans have absorbed the liquid and are tender.
2. Remove and discard the bay leaf.

Flavorful Cheese Soufflé Casserole

Prep time: 15 minutes | Cook time: 4-6 hours | Serves 4

- 14 slices fresh bread, crusts removed, divided
- 3 cups shredded sharp cheese, divided
- 2 tbsp. butter, melted, divided
- 6 eggs
- 3 cups milk, scalded
- 2 tsp. Worcestershire sauce
- ½ tsp. salt
- paprika

1. Tear bread into small pieces. Place half in well-greased slow cooker. Add half the shredded cheese and half the butter. Repeat layers.
2. Beat together eggs, milk, Worcestershire sauce, and salt. Pour over bread and cheese. Sprinkle top with paprika.
3. Cover. Cook on Low 4-6 hours.

Golden Garlic Rice

Prep time: 15 minutes |Cook time: 25 minutes|
Serves 4

- 1½ tablespoons Poached Garlic oil
- 1 cup long-grain white rice
- ¼ small yellow onion, finely chopped
- 3 Poached Garlic cloves, chopped
- 2 cups Very Easy Vegetable Broth or store bought
- ½ cup frozen mixed veggies
- ¼ cup sliced shiitake mushrooms

1. Add the oil, rice, onion, and garlic to a medium sauté pan. Cook over medium heat, stirring frequently, until the onions become translucent and the rice turns a golden brown (about 2 minutes).
2. Add the vegetable broth, frozen vegetables, and mushrooms.
3. Bring to a boil, cover, and lower to a simmer.
4. Allow to simmer for 20 minutes.

Quinoa with Vegetables

Prep time: 10 minutes | Cook time: 5-6 hours |
Serves 8

- 2 cups quinoa, rinsed and drained
- 2 onions, chopped
- 2 carrots, peeled and sliced
- 1 cup sliced cremini mushrooms
- 3 garlic cloves, minced
- 4 cups low-sodium vegetable broth
- ½ teaspoon salt
- 1 teaspoon dried marjoram leaves
- ⅛ teaspoon freshly ground black pepper

1. In a 6-quart slow cooker, mix all of the ingredients. Cover and cook on low for 5 to 6 hours, or until the quinoa and vegetables are tender.
2. Stir the mixture and serve.

Quinoa Ratatouille Casserole

Prep time: 10 minutes | Cook time: 8 hours |
Serves 4

- 1 teaspoon extra-virgin olive oil
- 1 cup diced eggplant
- 1 cup diced zucchini
- ½ teaspoon sea salt
- 1 (15-ounce) can whole plum tomatoes, undrained, hand-crushed
- 1 teaspoon minced garlic
- ½ cup minced onion
- 1 cup quinoa
- 1 teaspoon herbes de Provence
- 1½ cups low-sodium chicken or vegetable broth

1. Grease the inside of the slow cooker with the olive oil.
2. Put the eggplant and zucchini in a colander in the sink. Season them liberally with the salt and allow it to rest for 10 minutes, or up to 30 minutes if you have the time.
3. Put the tomatoes, garlic, onion, quinoa, herbes de Provence, and broth in the slow cooker.
4. Rinse the eggplant and zucchini under cool water and gently press any excess moisture from the salted vegetables before adding to them to the slow cooker. Mix everything thoroughly.
5. Cover and cook on low for 8 hours.

Vegetarian Baked Beans

Prep time: 10 minutes | Cook time: 1 1/2 hours | Serves 4

- 1 pound dried white navy beans
- 1/4 cup ketchup
- 1/4 cup pure maple syrup, preferably B grade
- 1/4 cup molasses
- 1 1/4 teaspoons dried summer or winter savory, or 2 1/2 teaspoons chopped fresh
- 1 teaspoon baking soda
- 1 teaspoon salt
- 1/4 teaspoon freshly ground black pepper
- 1 medium-size white onion, peeled, left whole, scored with an X at the root end, and studded with 4 cloves
- Boiling water to cover
- 1/2 cup (1 stick) butter or margarine, cut into pieces

1. Rinse the beans in a colander under cold running water; pick over for damaged beans and small stones. Transfer to the slow cooker. Cover with cold water by 2 inches, soak overnight, and drain.
2. Cover the beans with fresh water by 3 inches. Cover and cook on HIGH for 1 1/2 hours, until still undercooked. Drain.
3. Return the beans to the cooker and add the ketchup, maple syrup, molasses, savory, baking soda, salt, and pepper; stir to mix well. Press the whole onion down into the center of the beans. Add boiling water to cover by 1/2 inch; stir gently. Cover and cook on HIGH to bring to a boil, then reduce the heat to LOW and cook until the beans are soft, thick, and bubbling, 10 to 12 hours.
4. Remove the onion and stir in the butter until melted. Taste for seasoning and serve hot.

Meat-Free Lasagna

Prep time: 15 minutes | Cook time: 5 hours | Serves 8

- 4½ cups fat-free, low-sodium meatless spaghetti sauce
- ½ cup water
- 16-oz. container fat-free ricotta cheese
- 2 cups shredded part-skim mozzarella cheese, divided
- ¾ cup grated Parmesan cheese, divided
- 1 egg
- 2 tsp. minced garlic
- 1 tsp. Italian seasoning
- 8-oz. box no-cook lasagna noodles

1. Mix spaghetti sauce and ½ cup water in a bowl.
2. In a separate bowl, mix ricotta, 1½ cups mozzarella cheese, ½ cup Parmesan cheese, egg, garlic, and seasoning.
3. Spread ¼ of the sauce mixture in bottom of slow cooker. Top with ⅓ of the noodles, breaking if needed to fit.
4. Spread with ⅓ of the cheese mixture, making sure noodles are covered.
5. Repeat layers twice more.
6. Spread with remaining sauce.
7. Cover. Cook on Low 5 hours.
8. Sprinkle with remaining cheeses. Cover. Let stand 10 minutes to allow cheeses to melt.

Slow Cooker Almost Lasagna

Prep time: 40 minutes | Cook time: 4-6 hours | Serves 8-10

- 1 box rotini or ziti, cooked
- 2 tbsp. olive oil
- 2 28-oz. jars pasta sauce with tomato chunks
- 2 cups tomato juice
- ½ lb. ground beef
- ½ lb. bulk sausage, crumbled, or links cut into ¼-inch slices
- 1 cup Parmesan cheese
- ½ cup Italian bread crumbs
- 1 egg
- 2 cups mozzarella cheese, divided
- 2 cups ricotta cheese
- 2 eggs
- 1 cup Parmesan cheese
- 1½ tsp. parsley flakes
- ¾ tsp. salt
- ¼ tsp. pepper

1. In large bowl, toss pasta with olive oil. Add pasta sauce and tomato juice and mix well. Set aside.
2. Brown beef and sausage together in skillet. Drain.
3. Add 1 cup Parmesan cheese, bread crumbs, 1 egg, and 1 cup mozzarella cheese to meat. Set aside.
4. In separate bowl, beat together ricotta cheese, 2 eggs, 1 cup Parmesan cheese, parsley, salt, and pepper. Set aside.
5. Pour half of pasta-sauce mixture into slow cooker. Spread entire ricotta mixture over pasta. Top with entire meat-cheese mixture. Cover with remaining pasta-sauce mixture. Sprinkle with remaining 1 cup mozzarella cheese.
6. Cover. Cook on Low 4-6 hours.

Herbed Wild Rice

Prep time: 10 minutes | Cook time: 4-6 hours | Serves 8

- 3 cups wild rice, rinsed and drained
- 6 cups Roasted Vegetable Broth
- 1 onion, chopped
- ½ teaspoon salt
- ½ teaspoon dried thyme leaves
- ½ teaspoon dried basil leaves
- 1 bay leaf
- ⅓ cup chopped fresh flat-leaf parsley

1. In a 6-quart slow cooker, mix the wild rice, vegetable broth, onion, salt, thyme, basil, and bay leaf. Cover and cook on low for 4 to 6 hours, or until the wild rice is tender but still firm. You can cook this dish longer until the wild rice pops; that will take about 7 to 8 hours.
2. Remove and discard the bay leaf.
3. Stir in the parsley and serve.

Chapter 9

Vegan and Vegetarian

Scalloped Corn

Prep time: 10 minutes | Cook time: 3 to 6 hours | Serves 6

- 2 eggs
- 10¾-oz. can cream of celery soup
- ⅔ cup unseasoned bread crumbs
- 2 cups whole-kernel corn, drained, or cream-style corn
- 1 tsp. minced onion
- ¼–½ tsp. salt, according to your taste preference
- ⅛ tsp. pepper
- 1 tbsp. sugar
- 2 tbsp. butter, melted

1. Beat eggs with fork. Add soup and bread crumbs. Mix well.
2. Add remaining ingredients and mix thoroughly. Pour into greased slow cooker.
3. Cover. Cook on High 3 hours, or on Low 6 hours.

Broccoli Delight

Prep time: 15 minutes | Cook time: 2 to 6 hours | Serves 4-6

- 1-2 lbs. broccoli, chopped
- 2 cups cauliflower, chopped
- 10¾-oz. can 98% fat-free cream of celery soup
- ½ tsp. salt
- ¼ tsp. black pepper
- 1 medium onion, diced
- 2-4 garlic cloves, crushed, according to your taste preference
- ½ cup vegetable broth

1. Combine all ingredients in slow cooker.
2. Cook on Low 4-6 hours, or on High 2-3 hours.

Sweet and Sour Red Cabbage

Prep time: 20 minutes | Cook time: 5 to 7 hours | Serves 8

- 1 medium head red cabbage, cored and chopped about 8 cups
- 1 Granny Smith apple, peeled and chopped
- 1 red onion, chopped
- 3 tablespoons honey
- ¼ cup apple cider vinegar
- ½ teaspoon salt
- ⅛ teaspoon freshly ground black pepper
- pinch ground cloves

1. In a 6-quart slow cooker, mix all of the ingredients.
2. Cover and cook on low for 5 to 7 hours, or until the cabbage is very tender.

Golden Cauliflower

Prep time: 5-10 minutes | Cook time: 1½-5 hours | Serves 4-6

- 2 10-oz. pkgs. frozen cauliflower, thawed
- salt and pepper
- 10¾-oz. can condensed cheddar cheese soup
- 4 slices bacon, crisply fried and crumbled

1. Place cauliflower in slow cooker. Season with salt and pepper.
2. Spoon soup over top. Sprinkle with bacon.
3. Cover and cook on High 1½ hours, or on Low 4-5 hours, or until cauliflower is tender.

Braised Carrot-Maple Purée

Prep time: 20 minutes | Cook time: 6–8 hours | Serves 8

- 8 large carrots, peeled and sliced
- 1 red onion, chopped
- ¼ cup canned coconut milk
- 2 tablespoons grated fresh ginger root
- ¼ cup maple syrup
- ½ teaspoon salt

1. In a 6-quart slow cooker, mix all of the ingredients. Cover and cook on low for 6 to 8 hours, or until the carrots are very tender.
2. Using a potato masher or immersion blender, puree the mixture to the desired consistency.

Dried Corn

Prep time: 3–5 minutes | Cook time: 4 hours | Serves 4

- 15-oz. can dried corn
- 2 tbsp. sugar
- 3 tbsp. butter, softened
- 1 tsp. salt
- 1 cup half-and-half
- 2 tbsp. water

1. Place all ingredients in slow cooker. Mix together well.
2. Cover and cook on Low 4 hours. If you're able, check after cooking 3 hours to make sure the corn isn't cooking dry. If it appears to be, stir in an additional ¼–½ cup half-and-half. Cover and continue cooking.

Green Bean Casserole

Prep time: 10 minutes | Cook time: 3–10 hours | Makes 9–11

- 3 10-oz. pkgs. frozen, cut green beans
- 2 10½-oz. cans cheddar cheese soup
- ½ cup water
- ¼ cup chopped green onions
- 4-oz. can sliced mushrooms, drained
- ½ cup slivered almonds
- 1 tsp. salt
- ¼ tsp. pepper

1. Combine all ingredients in lightly greased slow cooker. Mix well.
2. Cover. Cook on Low 8–10 hours, or on High 3–4 hours.

Hearty Barbecued Beans

Prep time: 20 minutes | Cook time: 2–3 hours | Serves 10

- 1 lb. ground beef
- ½ cup chopped onions
- ½ tsp. salt
- ¼ tsp. pepper
- 28-oz. can pork and beans (your favorite variety)
- ½ cup ketchup
- 1 tbsp. Worcestershire sauce
- 1 tbsp. vinegar
- ¼ tsp. Tabasco sauce

1. Brown beef and onions together in skillet. Drain.
2. Combine all ingredients in slow cooker.
3. Cover. Cook on High 2–3 hours, stirring once or twice.
4. Serve with fresh raw vegetables and canned peaches.

Three-Cheese Macaroni

Prep time: 10 minutes | Cook time: 20 minutes | Serves 6

- 2 tablespoons unsalted butter
- ½ small yellow onion, diced
- 3 cups coarsely grated extra-sharp white cheddar cheese (12 ounces)
- 1 cup coarsely grated gruyère cheese (4 ounces)
- 12 ounces elbow macaroni
- 2 cups milk
- 2 cans (12 ounces each) evaporated milk
- 1 teaspoon dijon mustard
- ¼ teaspoon cayenne pepper (optional)
- coarse salt and freshly ground black pepper
- 1 ⅔ cups fresh breadcrumbs (see)
- ¼ cup finely grated parmigiano-reggiano cheese (1 ounce)

1. Melt 1 tablespoon butter in a small skillet over medium-high. Add onion and cook until softened, about 5 minutes.
2. Transfer onion to a 5- to 6-quart slow cooker. Add cheddar, Gruyère, macaroni, both milks, mustard, cayenne (if using), ½ teaspoon salt, and ¼ teaspoon black pepper.
3. Stir until macaroni is well coated and submerged in sauce. Cover and cook on low, 2 to 3 hours (or on high for 1 to 1½ hours).
4. In a skillet, melt remaining tablespoon butter over medium. Add breadcrumbs and toast, stirring often, until golden brown. Transfer to a bowl and mix in Parmigiano-Reggiano. Season with salt and black pepper.
5. In last 15 minutes of slow cooking, remove lid from cooker and sprinkle pasta with breadcrumbs.
6. Continue cooking, partially uncovered, until liquid is absorbed and top is golden brown. Season with salt and black pepper, and serve.

Tofu and Vegetables

Prep time: 20 minutes | Cook time: 6 hours | Serves 6

- 16 ozs. firm tofu, drained and crumbled
- ½ cup onion, chopped
- ½ cup celery, chopped
- 2 cups bok choy, chopped
- 2 cups napa cabbage, chopped
- ½ cup pea pods, cut in half

1. Combine all ingredients in slow cooker.
2. Cook on Low 6 hours.

Chilled Summer Berry Bisque

Prep time: 20 minutes | Cook time: none | Serves 8

- 4 ½ cups fresh or frozen blueberries, thawed, divided
- 1 cup unsweetened apple juice
- 1 cup orange juice
- ¼ cup honey
- 2 teaspoons minced fresh gingerroot
- 1 teaspoon grated orange peel
- ¼ teaspoon ground cinnamon
- ⅛ teaspoon ground nutmeg
- 2 cups (16 ounces) plain yogurt
- Fresh mint leaves

1. In a large saucepan, combine 4 cups blueberries, apple juice, orange juice, honey, ginger, orange peel, cinnamon and nutmeg. Bring to a boil, stirring occasionally. Cool slightly.
2. In a blender, process blueberry mixture and yogurt in batches until smooth. Refrigerate until chilled. Just before serving, garnish with mint and remaining blueberries.

Honey-Glazed Turnips

Prep time: 20 minutes | Cook time: 6-8 hours | Serves 8

- 4 pounds turnips, peeled and sliced
- 1 bulk fennel, cored and chopped
- 2 garlic cloves, minced
- ¼ cup honey
- ¼ cup Roasted Vegetable Broth
- ½ teaspoon salt
- 4 cups chopped turnip greens

1. In a 6-quart slow cooker, mix all of the ingredients.
2. Cover and cook on low for 6 to 8 hours, or until the turnips are tender when pierced with a fork and the greens are tender too.

Special Green Beans

Prep time: 30-45 minutes | Cook time: 1-2 hours | Serves 12-14

- 4 14½-oz. cans green beans, drained
- 10¾-oz. can cream of mushroom soup
- 14½-oz. can chicken broth
- 1 cup tater tots
- 3-oz. can French-fried onion rings

1. Put green beans in slow cooker.
2. In a bowl, mix soup and broth together. Spread over beans.
3. Spoon tater tots over all. Top with onion rings.
4. Cover and bake on High 1-2 hours, or until heated through and potatoes are cooked.

Summer Vegetable Tian

Prep time: 10 minutes | Cook time: 20 minutes | Serves 6

- 1 cup Tomato Sauce
- 1 zucchini, sliced ⅛ inch thick
- 3 baby eggplants, sliced ⅛ inch thick
- 3 firm plum tomatoes, sliced ⅛ inch thick
- 1 long red bell pepper, sliced ⅛ inch thick
- 1½ teaspoons chopped fresh thyme leaves
- ½ cup extra-virgin olive oil
- coarse salt and freshly ground pepper

1. Preheat a 5- to 6-quart slow cooker. Spread Tomato Sauce in bottom of the slow cooker.
2. In a large bowl, toss zucchini, eggplants, tomatoes, bell pepper, and thyme with 6 tablespoons oil; season with salt and pepper.
3. Stack slices of zucchini, eggplant, tomato, and pepper in piles, alternating vegetables. Lay stacks of vegetables on their sides in slow cooker, making a tight ring around the edge. Lay more vegetables down center, packing them tightly.
4. Drizzle remaining 2 tablespoons oil on top. Cover and cook on high until tender and bubbling, 3½ hours (or on low for 7 hours).
5. Tomato Sauce: Heat 1 tablespoon extra-virgin olive oil, 1 minced large garlic clove, and a pinch of red-pepper flakes in a pot over medium, stirring frequently, just until fragrant and sizzling, about 2 minutes.
6. Add 1 can (28 ounces) whole peeled tomatoes, chopped, and season with coarse salt and freshly ground black pepper. Bring to a boil over high heat; then reduce to a rapid simmer and cook, stirring occasionally and mashing tomatoes, until thickened, about 15 minutes.
7. Once cooled, sauce can be refrigerated in an airtight container up to 1 week; reheat over low before serving.

Chapter 10

Soups, Stews and Chilis

Chicken with Kale Leaves Soup

Prep time: 15 minutes | Cook time: 6 hours | Serves 6

- 2 lb. chicken breast
- 1/3 cup lime juice
- 1/3 cup onion finely chopped
- 3 tbsp olive oil
- 4 oz baby kale leaves
- 10 oz chicken broth

1. Using a large skillet, add in a tbsp of oil and heat over medium heat.
2. Cook the chicken for 15 minutes.
3. Once done, shred the chicken then transfer it into the slow cooker.
4. Pour the onions, chicken broth, and olive oil into a food processor and blend until well combined.
5. Pour the broth mix into the slow cooker, then add in the rest of the ingredients and stir.
6. Cover the pot then cook for 6 hours on low settings, occasionally stirring.
7. Serve and enjoy.

Cream of Fennel & Leek Soup

Prep time: 10 minutes | Cook time: 8 hours | Serves 4

- 1 teaspoon freshly ground fennel seed
- 1 fennel bulb, cored and chopped
- 1 leek, white and pale green parts only, sliced thin
- 1 white potato, peeled and diced
- ⅛ teaspoon sea salt
- 2 cups low-sodium chicken broth
- 1 teaspoon white wine vinegar or lemon juice
- 2 tablespoons heavy cream
- 1 sprig fresh tarragon, roughly chopped (optional)

1. Put the fennel seed, fennel bulb, leek, potato, salt, and broth in the slow cooker and stir to combine. Cover and cook on low for 8 hours.
2. Just before serving, add the vinegar to the crock and then purée the soup with an immersion blender. Stir in the heavy cream.
3. Serve garnished with fresh tarragon (if using).

Turkey-Vegetable Stew

Prep time: 20 minutes | Cook time: 7 to 8 hours on low | Serves 6

- 3 tablespoons extra-virgin olive oil, divided
- 1 pound boneless turkey breast, cut into 1-inch pieces
- 1 leek, thoroughly cleaned and sliced
- 2 teaspoons minced garlic
- 2 cups chicken broth
- 1 cup coconut milk
- 2 celery stalks, chopped
- 2 cups diced pumpkin
- 1 carrot, diced
- 2 teaspoons chopped thyme
- salt, for seasoning
- freshly ground black pepper, for seasoning
- 1 scallion, white and green parts, chopped, for garnish

1. Lightly grease the insert of the slow cooker with 1 tablespoon of the olive oil.
2. In a large skillet over medium-high heat, heat the remaining 2 tablespoons of the olive oil. Add the turkey and sauté until browned, about 5 minutes.
3. Add the leek and garlic and sauté for an additional 3 minutes.
4. Transfer the turkey mixture to the insert and stir in the broth, coconut milk, celery, pumpkin, carrot, and thyme.
5. Cover and cook on low for 7 to 8 hours.
6. Season with salt and pepper.
7. Serve topped with the scallion.

Poached Garlic and Potato Soup

Prep time: 10 minutes |Cook time: 6 to 8 hours|
Serves 6

- ¾ cup Poached Garlic cloves, minced
- 4 cups diced potatoes
- 2 cups frozen broccoli
- ½ medium yellow onion, diced
- 6 cups Very Easy Vegetable Broth or store bought
- Juice of ½ lemon
- ½ teaspoon salt
- Freshly ground black pepper
- Splash hot sauce (optional)

1. Place the garlic, potatoes, broccoli, onion, vegetable broth, lemon juice, and salt in a slow cooker. Season with pepper and hot sauce (if using), and stir well.
2. Cover and cook on low for 6 to 8 hours or on high for 4 to 6 hours.
3. Use an immersion blender (or a traditional blender) to blend about two-thirds of the soup (or to your desired consistency).

Pumpkin Black Bean Chili

Prep time: 10 minutes | Cook time: 8 hours |
Serves 4

- 1 cup canned black beans, drained and rinsed
- 1 cup canned fire-roasted diced tomatoes, drained
- 1 cup unsweetened pumpkin purée
- ½ cup diced onion
- ½ cup diced green bell pepper
- 1 teaspoon minced garlic
- 1 teaspoon ground Ancho chile
- 1 teaspoon smoked paprika
- ⅛ teaspoon cinnamon
- ⅛ teaspoon sea salt
- ¼ cup shredded Cheddar cheese, for garnish

- 2 tablespoons sour cream, for garnish
- ¼ cup roughly chopped fresh cilantro, for garnish

1. Put the beans, tomatoes, pumpkin, onion, bell pepper, garlic, chili powder, paprika, cinnamon, and salt in the slow cooker, and stir to combine.
2. Cover and cook on low for 8 hours.
3. Garnish each serving with the Cheddar cheese, sour cream, and fresh cilantro.

Southern Paleo Slow Cooker Chili

Prep time: 10 minutes | Cook time: 8 hours | Serves 6

- 1 lb. organic beef
- 20 oz tomatoes, chopped
- 3 chopped carrots
- 1 tsp onion powder
- 1 tsp paprika
- 1 diced onion
- 1 tsp garlic powder
- 1 tbsp Worcestershire sauce
- 1 tbsp fresh parsley, chopped
- 1 seeded & diced green bell pepper
- 3 tsp chili powder

1. Using a medium-sized skillet, add in the ground beef and brown over high heat, occasionally stirring until there is no pink.
2. Put the browned beef inside the slow cooker, including the fat.
3. Add in the onion, green bell pepper, tomatoes, and carrots into the slow cooker.
4. Mix all the fixing, then put in all the remaining seasonings and spices.
5. Stir all the ingredients together again, then cover and cook for 8 hours on low settings or 5 on high settings.
6. Serve then top with sour cream and jalapenos and enjoy.

Spring-Thyme Chicken Stew

Prep time: 15 minutes | Cook time: 7 hours | Serves 4

- 1 pound small red potatoes, halved
- 1 large onion, finely chopped
- $^3/_4$ cup shredded carrots
- 3 tablespoons all-purpose flour
- 6 garlic cloves, minced
- 2 teaspoons grated lemon peel
- 2 teaspoons dried thyme
- $^1/_2$ teaspoon salt
- $^1/_4$ teaspoon pepper
- 1 $^1/_2$ pounds boneless skinless chicken thighs, halved
- 2 cups reduced-sodium chicken broth
- 2 bay leaves
- 2 tablespoons minced fresh parsley

1. Place potatoes, onion and carrots in a 3-qt. slow cooker. Sprinkle with flour, garlic, lemon peel, thyme, salt and pepper; toss to coat. Place chicken over top. Add broth and bay leaves.
2. Cook, covered, on low 7-9 hours or until chicken and vegetables are tender. Remove bay leaves. Sprinkle with parsley.

Simple Texas Chili

Prep time: 20 minutes | Cook time: 7 to 8 hours on low | Serves 4

- ¼ cup extra-virgin olive oil
- 1½ pounds beef sirloin, cut into 1-inch chunks
- 1 sweet onion, chopped
- 2 green bell peppers, chopped
- 1 jalapeño pepper, seeded, finely chopped
- 2 teaspoons minced garlic
- 1 (28-ounce) can diced tomatoes
- 1 cup beef broth
- 3 tablespoons chili powder
- ½ teaspoon ground cumin
- ¼ teaspoon ground coriander
- 1 cup sour cream, for garnish
- 1 avocado, diced, for garnish
- 1 tablespoon cilantro, chopped, for garnish

1. Lightly grease the insert of the slow cooker with 1 tablespoon of the olive oil.
2. In a large skillet over medium-high heat, heat the remaining 2 tablespoons of the olive oil. Add the beef and sauté until it is cooked through, about 8 minutes.
3. Add the onion, bell peppers, jalapeño pepper, and garlic, and sauté for an additional 4 minutes.
4. Transfer the beef mixture to the insert and stir in the tomatoes, broth, chili powder, cumin, and coriander.
5. Cover and cook on low for 7 to 8 hours.
6. Serve topped with the sour cream, avocado, and cilantro.

Sweet Spiced Lentil Soup

Prep time: 10 minutes | Cook time: 8 hours | Serves 4

- 1 cup dried lentils, rinsed and sorted
- 1 apple, cored, peeled, and diced
- 1 cup diced onion
- ¼ cup diced celery
- 1 teaspoon fresh thyme
- ¼ teaspoon ground cinnamon
- ¼ teaspoon ground allspice
- ⅛ teaspoon sea salt
- ¼ cup dry red wine
- 3 cups low-sodium chicken or vegetable broth

1. Put all the ingredients into the slow cooker and stir to combine.
2. Cover and cook on low for 6 to 8 hours, until the lentils are very soft.

Miso Vegetable Soup

Prep time: 15 minutes |Cook time: 7 to 8 hours| Serves 4

- 6 cups Very Easy Vegetable Broth or store bought
- 1 tablespoon white miso paste
- ½ head napa cabbage, chopped
- 2 carrots, scrubbed and sliced
- 1 celery stalk, diced
- 1 teaspoon minced garlic (2 cloves)
- 1 (½-inch) piece fresh ginger, peeled and minced
- ¼ teaspoon red pepper flakes (optional)
- ½ package rice noodles (about 4 ounces, optional)

1. Combine the vegetable broth, miso paste, cabbage, carrots, celery, garlic, ginger, and red pepper flakes (if using) in a slow cooker. Stir to combine.
2. Cover and cook for 7 to 8 hours on low or 3 to 4 hours on high.
3. If using the rice noodles, add them to the slow cooker 20 minutes before serving.

Minestrone Soup

Prep time: 15 minutes |Cook time: 6 hours| Serves 4

- 6 cups Very Easy Vegetable Broth or store bought
- 1 (14.5-ounce) can diced tomatoes, with juice
- 2 carrots, scrubbed, halved, and sliced
- 2 celery stalks, sliced
- 2 medium Yukon or red potatoes, diced
- 1 cup frozen broccoli or green beans
- 1 medium yellow onion, diced
- 2 teaspoons minced garlic (4 cloves)
- 2 cups stemmed, chopped kale
- 1 (15-ounce) can red kidney beans, drained and rinsed

- 1 (15-ounce) can black beans, drained and rinsed
- 1 (8-ounce) can tomato sauce
- 1 teaspoon dried oregano
- 1 teaspoon ground cumin
- 2 bay leaves
- 1 cup small tubular or elbow pasta

1. Place the vegetable broth, diced tomatoes, carrots, celery, potatoes, broccoli or green beans, onion, garlic, kale, kidney beans, black beans, tomato sauce, oregano, cumin, and bay leaves in a slow cooker. Mix well.
2. Cover and cook on low for 5 hours, 45 minutes.
3. Turn the slow cooker to high, add the pasta, and continue to cook for 15 minutes more, or until the pasta is tender.

Chapter 11

Desserts

Almonds, Walnuts & Mango Bowls

Prep time: 10 minutes | Cook time: 2 hours | Serves 2

- 1 cup walnuts, chopped
- 3 tbsp almonds, chopped
- 1 cup mango, peeled and roughly cubed
- 1 cup heavy cream
- ½ tsp vanilla extract
- 1 tsp almond extract
- 2 tbsp brown sugar

1. In your slow cooker, mix the nuts with the mango, cream and the other ingredients, toss, put the lid on and cook on High for 2 hours.
2. Divide the mix into bowls and serve.

Red Raspberry Fruit Punch

Prep time: 5-10 minutes | Cook time: 1 hour | Makes 10 1-cup

- 1 quart cranberry juice
- 3 cups water
- 6-oz. can frozen orange juice concentrate, thawed
- 10-oz. pkg. frozen red raspberries, thawed
- 2 oranges, sliced
- 6 sticks cinnamon
- 12 whole allspice

1. Combine all ingredients in slow cooker.
2. Heat on High 1 hour, or until hot. Turn to Low while serving.

Fresh Cream Mix

Prep time: 1 hour | Cook time: 1 hour | Serves 6

- 1 ½ cup fresh cream
- 1 tsp cinnamon powder
- 3 egg yolks
- 2 tbsp white sugar
- Zest of 1 orange, grated

- a pinch of nutmeg for serving
- 2 tbsp sugar
- 1 ½ cup water

1. In a bowl, mix cream, cinnamon and orange zest and stir.
2. In another bowl, mix the egg yolks with white sugar and whisk well.
3. Add this over the cream, stir, strain and divide into ramekins.
4. Put ramekins in your slow cooker, add 2 cups water to the slow cooker, cover, cook on Low for 1 hour, leave cream aside to cool down and serve.

Pears and Apples Bowls

Prep time: 10 minutes | Cook time: 2 hours | Serves 2

- 1 tsp vanilla extract
- 2 pears, cored and cut into wedges
- 2 apples, cored and cut into wedges
- 1 tbsp walnuts, chopped
- 2 tbsp brown sugar
- ½ cup coconut cream

1. In your slow cooker, mix the pears with the apples, nuts and the other ingredients, toss, put the lid on and cook on Low for 2 hours.
2. Divide the mix into bowls and serve cold.

Chunky Applesauce

Prep time: 10 minutes | Cook time: 3-10 hours | Serves 8-10

- 8 apples, peeled, cored, and cut into chunks or slices (6 cups)
- 1 tsp. cinnamon
- ½ cup water
- ½-1 cup sugar or cinnamon red hot candies

1. Combine all ingredients in slow cooker.
2. Cook on Low 8-10 hours, or on High 3-4 hours.

Pumpkin Pie Pudding

Prep time: 10 minutes | Cook time: 3 hours | Serves 8

- 15-oz. can pumpkin
- 12-oz. can evaporated skim milk
- ¾ cup Splenda
- ½ cup low-fat buttermilk baking mix
- 2 eggs, beaten, or 6 egg whites
- 2 tsp. pumpkin pie spice
- 1 tsp. lemon zest

1. Combine all ingredients in slow cooker sprayed with cooking spray. Stir until lumps disappear.
2. Cover. Cook on Low 3 hours.
3. Serve warm or cold.

Chocolate, Berry, and Macadamia Jars

Prep time: 15 minutes | Cook time: 6 hours | Serves 6

- 6 oz dark chocolate, melted
- ½ cup mixed berries, (fresh) – any berries you like
- 3/4 cup toasted macadamia nuts, chopped
- 6 oz cream cheese
- ½ cup heavy cream

- 1 tsp vanilla extract

1. Whisk the cream cheese, cream, and vanilla extract in a medium-sized bowl.
2. Scoop a small amount of melted chocolate, put it into each jar or ramekin.
3. Place a few berries on top of the chocolate.
4. Sprinkle some toasted macadamias onto the berries.
5. Scoop the cream cheese mixture into the ramekin.
6. Place another layer of chocolate, berries, and macadamia nuts on top of the cream cheese mixture.
7. Put the jars inside the slow cooker and put the hot water until it reaches halfway up.
8. Set to low, then cook for 6 hours.
9. Remove the jars and leave them to cool and set on the bench for about 2 hours before serving.

Black and Blue Cobbler

Prep time: 20 minutes | Cook time: 2-2½ hours | Serves 6

- 1 cup flour
- ¾ cup sugar
- 1 tsp. baking powder
- ¼ tsp. salt
- ¼ tsp. ground cinnamon
- ¼ tsp. ground nutmeg
- 2 eggs, beaten
- 2 tbsp. milk
- 2 tbsp. vegetable oil
- 2 cups fresh or frozen blueberries
- 2 cups fresh or frozen blackberries
- ¾ cup water
- 1 tsp. grated orange peel
- ¾ cup sugar
- whipped topping or ice cream, optional

1. Combine flour, ¾ cup sugar, baking powder, salt, cinnamon, and nutmeg.
2. Combine eggs, milk, and oil. Stir into dry ingredients until moistened.
3. Spread the batter evenly over bottom of greased 5-quart slow cooker.
4. In saucepan, combine berries, water, orange peel, and ¾ cup sugar. Bring to boil. Remove from heat and pour over batter. Cover.
5. Cook on High 2-2½ hours, or until toothpick inserted into batter comes out clean. Turn off cooker.
6. Uncover and let stand 30 minutes before serving. Spoon from cooker and serve with whipped topping or ice cream, if desired.

Cranberry Pudding

Prep time: 20 minutes | Cook time: 3-4 hours | Serves 8-10

Pudding:

- 1⅓ cups flour
- ½ tsp. salt
- 2 tsp. baking soda
- ⅓ cup boiling water
- ½ cup dark molasses
- 2 cups whole cranberries
- ½ cup chopped nuts
- ½ cup water

Butter Sauce:

- 1 cup confectioners sugar
- ½ cup heavy cream or evaporated milk
- ½ cup butter
- 1 tsp. vanilla

1. Mix together flour and salt.
2. Dissolve soda in boiling water. Add to flour and salt.
3. Stir in molasses. Blend well.
4. Fold in cranberries and nuts.
5. Pour into well greased and floured bread or cake pan that will sit in your cooker. Cover with greased foil.
6. Pour ½ cup water into cooker. Place foil-covered pan in cooker. Cover with cooker lid and steam on High 3 to 4 hours, or until pudding tests done with a wooden pick.
7. Remove pan and uncover. Let stand 5 minutes, then unmold.
8. To make butter sauce, mix together all ingredients in saucepan. Cook, stirring over medium heat until sugar dissolves.
9. Serve warm butter sauce over warm cranberry pudding.

Hot Spicy Lemonade Punch

Prep time: 5–10 minutes | Cook time: 3–4 hours | Makes 9–10 1-cup

- 4 cups cranberry juice
- ⅓–⅔ cup sugar
- 12-oz. can lemonade concentrate, thawed
- 4 cups water
- 1–2 tbsp. honey
- 6 whole cloves
- 2 cinnamon sticks, broken
- 1 lemon, sliced

1. Combine juice, sugar, lemonade, water, and honey in slow cooker.
2. Tie cloves and cinnamon in small cheesecloth square. Add spice bag and lemon slices to slow cooker.
3. Cover and cook on Low 3–4 hours. Remove spice bag. Keep hot in slow cooker until ready to serve.

Apple-Nut Bread Pudding

Prep time: 15 minutes | Cook time: 3–4 hours | Serves 6–8

- 8 slices raisin bread, cubed
- 2–3 medium tart apples, peeled and sliced
- 1 cup chopped pecans, toasted
- 1 cup sugar
- 1 tsp. ground cinnamon
- ½ tsp. ground nutmeg
- 3 eggs, lightly beaten
- 2 cups half-and-half
- ¼ cup apple juice
- ¼ cup butter, melted

1. Place bread cubes, apples, and pecans in greased slow cooker and mix together gently.
2. Combine sugar, cinnamon, and nutmeg. Add remaining ingredients. Mix well. Pour over bread mixture.
3. Cover. Cook on Low 3–4 hours, or until

knife inserted in center comes out clean.

4. Serve with ice cream.

Easy Chocolate Clusters

Prep time: 5 minutes|Cook time: 2 hours |Makes 3½ dozen clusters

- 2 lbs. white coating chocolate, broken into small pieces
- 2 cups (12 oz.) semisweet chocolate chips
- 4-oz. pkg. sweet German chocolate
- 24-oz. jar roasted peanuts

1. Combine coating chocolate, chocolate chips, and German chocolate. Cover and cook on High 1 hour. Reduce heat to Low and cook 1 hour longer, or until chocolate is melted, stirring every 15 minutes.
2. Stir in peanuts. Mix well.
3. Drop by teaspoonfuls onto waxed paper. Let stand until set. Store at room temperature.

Slow Cooker Chocolate Caramel Monkey Bread

Prep time: 15 minutes | Cook time: 1 hour 30 minutes | Serves 6

- 1 tbsp sugar
- 1/4 tsp ground cinnamon
- 15 oz buttermilk biscuits
- 18 milk chocolate-covered caramels
- caramel sauce for topping (optional)
- chocolate sauce for topping (optional)

1. Mix sugar and cinnamon and set aside.
2. Fill a parchment paper slow cooker, cover up to the bottom.
3. Wrap 1 buttermilk biscuit dough around one chocolate candy to cover the candy completely, pinching the seam closed.
4. Place the biscuit-wrapped candy in the slow cooker bottom, start in the middle of the slow cooker and work your way to the sides.
5. Continue to wrap candy and put it in the slow cooker, leaving roughly 1/2 inch between each.
6. Repeat these steps with sweets wrapped in the second layer of biscuit.
7. Sprinkle the remaining cinnamon-sugar mixture on top when using all the dough and confectionery.
8. Cover the slow cooker and cook for 1 1/2 hours on the lower side.
9. Once cooked, remove the lid and let cool slightly.
10. Use the edges of the parchment paper to lift the monkey bread out of the slow cooker.
11. Allow cooling for at least 10-15 minutes.
12. Cut off any excess parchment paper around the edge when ready to serve.
13. In a shallow bread or bowl, put monkey bread and drizzle with chocolate and caramel sauces.

Bread Pudding

Prep time: 20 minutes | Cook time: 4-5 hours | Serves 6

- 8 slices bread (raisin bread is especially good), cubed
- 4 eggs
- 2 cups milk
- ¼ cup sugar
- ¼ cup butter, melted
- ½ cup raisins (use only ¼ cup if using raisin bread)
- ½ tsp. cinnamon

Sauce:
- 2 tbsp. butter
- 2 tbsp. flour
- 1 cup water
- ¾ cup sugar
- 1 tsp. Vanilla

1. Place bread cubes in greased slow cooker.
2. Beat together eggs and milk. Stir in sugar, butter, raisins, and cinnamon. Pour over bread and stir.
3. Cover and cook on High 1 hour. Reduce heat to Low and cook 3-4 hours, or until thermometer reaches 160°.
4. Make sauce just before pudding is done baking. Begin by melting butter in saucepan. Stir in flour until smooth. Gradually add water, sugar, and vanilla. Bring to boil. Cook, stirring constantly for 2 minutes, or until thickened.
5. Serve sauce over warm bread pudding.

Appendix 1 Measurement Conversion Chart

Volume Equivalents (Dry)

US STANDARD	METRIC (APPROXIMATE)
1/8 teaspoon	0.5 mL
1/4 teaspoon	1 mL
1/2 teaspoon	2 mL
3/4 teaspoon	4 mL
1 teaspoon	5 mL
1 tablespoon	15 mL
1/4 cup	59 mL
1/2 cup	118 mL
3/4 cup	177 mL
1 cup	235 mL
2 cups	475 mL
3 cups	700 mL
4 cups	1 L

Volume Equivalents (Liquid)

US STANDARD	US STANDARD (OUNCES)	METRIC (APPROXIMATE)
2 tablespoons	1 fl.oz.	30 mL
1/4 cup	2 fl.oz.	60 mL
1/2 cup	4 fl.oz.	120 mL
1 cup	8 fl.oz.	240 mL
1 1/2 cup	12 fl.oz.	355 mL
2 cups or 1 pint	16 fl.oz.	475 mL
4 cups or 1 quart	32 fl.oz.	1 L
1 gallon	128 fl.oz.	4 L

Temperatures Equivalents

FAHRENHEIT(F)	CELSIUS(C) APPROXIMATE
225 °F	107 °C
250 °F	120 ° °C
275 °F	135 °C
300 °F	150 °C
325 °F	160 °C
350 °F	180 °C
375 °F	190 °C
400 °F	205 °C
425 °F	220 °C
450 °F	235 °C
475 °F	245 °C
500 °F	260 °C

Weight Equivalents

US STANDARD	METRIC (APPROXIMATE)
1 ounce	28 g
2 ounces	57 g
5 ounces	142 g
10 ounces	284 g
15 ounces	425 g
16 ounces (1 pound)	455 g
1.5 pounds	680 g
2 pounds	907 g

Appendix 2 The Dirty Dozen and Clean Fifteen

The Environmental Working Group (EWG) is a nonprofit, nonpartisan organization dedicated to protecting human health and the environment Its mission is to empower people to live healthier lives in a healthier environment. This organization publishes an annual list of the twelve kinds of produce, in sequence, that have the highest amount of pesticide residue-the Dirty Dozen-as well as a list of the fifteen kinds ofproduce that have the least amount of pesticide residue-the Clean Fifteen.

THE DIRTY DOZEN	
The 2016 Dirty Dozen includes the following produce. These are considered among the year's most important produce to buy organic:	

Strawberries	Spinach
Apples	Tomatoes
Nectarines	Bell peppers
Peaches	Cherry tomatoes
Celery	Cucumbers
Grapes	Kale/collard greens
Cherries	Hot peppers

The Dirty Dozen list contains two additional itemskale/collard greens and hot peppers-because they tend to contain trace levels of highly hazardous pesticides.

THE CLEAN FIFTEEN	
The least critical to buy organically are the Clean Fifteen list. The following are on the 2016 list:	

Avocados	Papayas
Corn	Kiw
Pineapples	Eggplant
Cabbage	Honeydew
Sweet peas	Grapefruit
Onions	Cantaloupe
Asparagus	Cauliflower
Mangos	

Some of the sweet corn sold in the United States are made from genetically engineered (GE) seedstock. Buy organic varieties of these crops to avoid GE produce.

Appendix 3 Index

Shelly J. Wilkerson